Receiving
Jesus

Receiving Jesus
The Way of Love

MARIANN EDGAR BUDDE

CHURCH
PUBLISHING
INCORPORATED

For the people
of the Episcopal Diocese
of Washington

Church Publishing
19 East 34th Street
New York, NY 10016
www.churchpublishing.org

Cover design by Jennifer Kopec, 2Pug Design
Typeset by Rose Design

Library of Congress Cataloging-in-Publication Data

Names: Budde, Mariann Edgar, 1959– author.
Title: Receiving Jesus : the way of love / Mariann Edgar Budde ; foreword
   by Michael B. Curry.
Description: New York : Church Publishing, 2019.
Identifiers: LCCN 2019017931 (print) | LCCN 2019981029 (ebook) | ISBN
   9781640652408 (pbk.) | ISBN 9781640652415 (ebook)
Subjects: LCSH: Spirituality—Christianity. | Spiritual life—Christianity.
   | Christian life. | Love—Religious aspects—Christianity.
Classification: LCC BV4501.3 .B834 2019 (print) | LCC BV4501.3 (ebook) |
   DDC 241/.4—dc23
LC record available at https://lccn.loc.gov/2019017931
LC ebook record available at https://lccn.loc.gov/2019981029

CONTENTS

FOREWORD

I AM UNAPOLOGETIC in admitting that I am "a one-note Char-
lie" when it comes to proclaiming the love of God. Indeed, I mean
it when I say that if it is not about love, it's not about God! This
love—intentional, unconditional, sacrificial—is the heart and soul
of the message of Jesus. And in Jesus we see the very heart of God!

In the initial days following the royal wedding of the Duke and
Duchess of Sussex, one interviewer surprised me with a great question, "Does this love you are preaching really work?" My answer
both then and now is an unequivocal "Yes"—Love is the *only* thing
that really works. It is the force behind all that has proven good
and true in the world. And because of that, choosing the Way of
Love is choosing to live life as it is meant to be lived, as nothing less
than God's dream for us and our world.

But there is another question that is also worth asking: *How do
we live this Way of Love?* It is this question that the Rt. Rev. Mariann Budde, bishop of Washington, answers so clearly and so beautifully in the following pages. Here you will be introduced to seven
steps, seven intentional practices—to Turn, Learn, Pray, Worship,
Bless, Go, Rest—that are part of what she appropriately calls the
journey of a lifetime. Through stories both personal and poignant,
she makes this journey real.

Let me be perfectly clear. As I turned these pages, I found that
Bishop Mariann did more than make me think; she captured my
heart's desire. For here I discovered anew the unconditional love of
God that Jesus taught in an intimate, personal way. Here is a Way

that can change our lives for the good, and through us our society and the entire global community. She has put heart, soul, and feet to the Jesus Movement.

So don't hesitate . . . dive in, immerse yourself in this Way of Love, and claim it for yourself.

You will be so glad you did.

THE MOST REV. MICHAEL BRUCE CURRY
XXVII PRESIDING BISHOP & PRIMATE
OF THE EPISCOPAL CHURCH

INTRODUCTION

Jesus said "I am the true vine, and my Father is the vine-grower. He removes every branch in me that bears no fruit. Every branch that bears fruit he prunes to make it bear more fruit. You have already been cleansed by the word that I have spoken to you. Abide in me as I abide in you. Just as the branch cannot bear fruit by itself unless it abides in the vine, neither can you unless you abide in me." —John 15:1–4

IN DECEMBER 2017 the presiding bishop of the Episcopal Church, Michael Curry, invited a small group of Episcopal Church leaders to help him think through an issue that was troubling him.

We in the Episcopal Church have been inspired by Bishop Curry's preaching for years, long before his sermon at the royal wedding of Prince Harry and Meghan Markle catapulted his message of love onto the world stage. Since his election as our presiding bishop in 2015, he has been preaching and teaching around the country, calling upon every member of the Episcopal Church to renew our commitment to Jesus and his message of love for the world. The energy around the presiding bishop, both within and outside the Episcopal Church, has been electrifying. Presiding Bishop Curry wants only to speak of Jesus, the one sent by God to show us all how to live and how to love. He is, in essence, a one-man revival. "The church is not an institution," he reminds us any chance he gets, "the church is a movement." Every time he speaks, we in the Episcopal Church cheer. But what exactly does that mean?

At our December 2017 gathering, Michael Curry wanted to talk about evangelism strategy. For while there are shining examples of spiritual vitality and growth in some Episcopal churches across the country, many of our congregations are struggling simply to survive. Even when we consider the strongest of our churches, the overall trends of decline are sobering. Despite Bishop Curry's current public stature, in the United States the majority of people under the age of fifty have no idea who we are and what our deepest hopes are for our world. Sadly, the treasure of the Episcopal Church, for many, remains hidden under the bushel basket of institutional decline.

Thus for two days we prayed and wondered together how best to be faithful to Jesus and his movement. What more could the presiding bishop do? What could we do, not merely to ensure the mere survival of our churches, but that they might thrive as vibrant spiritual communities and compelling witnesses to Jesus's message of love?

Part of the problem, we told ourselves, is that Episcopalians are hesitant to speak about our faith. We almost never invite our friends and neighbors to join us in worship or small group gatherings. Moreover, we seem inordinately attached to our preferences in worship. We like to think of church communities as warm, welcoming, and inclusive, but given our institutional decline, it is highly unlikely that others experience us that way. At our gathering, we acknowledged that the trends of decline suggest that the Episcopal Church is not a particularly compelling witness to the gospel. Clearly, we need to do more than trying harder to make our presence known and be more welcoming.

After hours of conversation, someone in our group asked the presiding bishop what concerned him most. "I worry," Presiding Bishop Curry said quietly, "that the majority of people in our churches do not know for themselves the unconditional love of God. I suspect that the reason they are hesitant to speak of Jesus is because they don't know him as their personal Lord and Savior." He paused. "How can we share what we don't have?"

The room went silent. I found myself thinking back to something I had recently read of how Christians experience the Holy Spirit in a book on the essentials of the Christian faith by Methodist pastor Adam Hamilton:

> When we speak about the Holy Spirit, or the Spirit of God, we are speaking of God's active work in our lives; of God's way of leading us, guiding us, forming and shaping us; of God's power and presence to comfort and encourage us and to make us the people God wants us to be. The Spirit is the voice of God whispering, wooing and beckoning us. And in listening to this voice and being shaped by this power, we find that we become most fully and authentically human.[1]

Hamilton goes on:

> I think that many Christians live Spirit-deficient lives, a bit like someone who is sleep-deprived, nutrient-deprived, or oxygen-deprived. Many Christians haven't been taught about the Spirit, nor encouraged to seek the Spirit's work in their lives. As a result, our spiritual lives are a bit anemic as we try living the Christian life by our own power and wisdom.[2]

As I heard the presiding bishop speak and recalled Adam Hamilton's words, it was as if God were holding a mirror to my face. I had to acknowledge to myself and before God that on most days, I try to live and lead from my own power and wisdom. In over thirty years of ordained leadership, my daily default position is to assume that everything depends on me. Intellectually, I know that's not the gospel. Never once does Jesus say, "It's all up to you." Rather he says things like, "I am the vine; you are the branches." He is the source

---

1. Adam Hamilton, *Creed: What Christians Believe and Why* (Nashville: Abingdon Press, 2016), Kindle Edition, 965.
2. Ibid, 1066.

of our strength. We are the branches, only able to share what we receive from him. Yet knowledge isn't enough: as a Christian—and most certainly as a leader of other Christians—I need daily reminders, and lived experiece, of the fundamental truth that apart from Jesus, I can do nothing.

Bishop Curry told us that he wants to spend his remaining years as our spiritual leader helping all people experience the love of God made known to us in Jesus, and to follow Jesus in that way of love. He wants the Episcopal Church to be known for our commitment to follow in Jesus's way of love. We were unanimous in our desire to join in that endeavor; together we dreamed of what a spiritual rule of life for the Episcopal Church might look like. The circle soon grew wider to include among the most gifted teachers, writers, and preachers in the Episcopal Church. From an extraordinarily rich collaborative endeavor, *The Way of Love: Practices for a Jesus-Centered Life* was born.

A Spiritual Rule of Life

The term, "a rule of life," is simply religious language for something we all do whenever we decide to direct intentional effort toward an overarching goal. The kind of goal that a rule of life points to isn't an accomplishment, but rather a way of being in the world. For example, in an academic setting, while it's possible to pass an exam by furiously studying the night before, mastery of a given subject matter requires continual study over time. A rule of life means following daily practices that would lead to such mastery. In the realm of physical health, while it's possible to lose weight on a starvation diet, sustained health requires daily habits of proper eating and exercise. Those habits constitute a rule of life for our health. Similarly, if we want to have a healthy relationship with money, a financial rule of life would entail adopting a budget and living within its means.

A spiritual rule of life is comprised of specific practices that help us pay attention and respond to the presence of God. It is a conscious effort on our part to be open to the love of God in Jesus, to receive that love for ourselves, and then offer love to others as we feel called. If we adhere to a few essential spiritual practices over time, they gradually shape our character and determine the course of our lives.

The writer Brian McLaren describes the power of spiritual practices this way:

> Spiritual practices are those actions within our power that help us narrow the gap between the character we want to have and the character we are actually developing. They're about surviving our twenties or forties or eighties and not becoming a jerk in the process. About not letting what happens to us deform or destroy us. About realizing that what we earn or accumulate means nothing compared to what we become and who we are. Spiritual practices are about life, about training ourselves to become the kinds of people who have eyes and actually see, and who have ears and actually hear, and so experience not just survival but life that is real, worth living, and good.[3]

McLaren goes on to say that our character—the kind of people we are—determines how much of God we can experience, and maybe even which version of God we experience. Thus, there's a lot at stake here for us, for it is through spiritual practices that we learn to love God.[4]

The primary goal of the Way of Love is for us to grow in our love for Jesus as we experience his love for us. The second is to grow in our capacity to love others as Jesus loves. The kind of

---

3. Brian McLaren, *Finding Our Way Again: The Return of the Ancient Practices* (Nashville: Thomas Nelson, 2008), 14.

4. Ibid., 18.

love we're aiming for isn't a feeling that washes over us, as wonderful as that feeling of love can be. Rather, it is sustained and sometimes sacrificial effort. In the words of Paul, this is love that is patient and kind; love that is not arrogant or boastful or rude; love that believes, hopes and endures all things; love that never ends (1 Cor. 13:1–13). Growing in our capacity to both receive and offer such love is the fruit of a life that is connected to love of Jesus, as a branch is to the vine. The practices of the Way of Love help us stay connected.

If we're honest, most of us feel inadequate when it comes to the disciplines of our faith. I know that I do. But here's something to remember about spiritual practices: they aren't meant to be chores to plow through or exercises to whip us into spiritual shape. In the words of the Benedictine nun Joan Chittister, "A relationship with God is not something to be achieved." Rather, she writes, "God is a presence to which we can respond." Nor is the spiritual life separate from the rest of our lives, but rather, "a way of being in the world that is open to God and open to others."[5] Spiritual practices help open us to God's presence.

The seven practices of the Way of Love are not, for the most part, dramatic gestures, but rather small steps we take whose impact will be felt over time. Nor is this a program explicitly designed to fix the challenges we face as a church in institutional decline. There is no guarantee that even if every Episcopalian decided to follow the Way of Love that we would reverse the trends of shrinking membership. On the other hand, if we never engage in these practices, or others like them, we may not have a church worth saving. The church isn't a building, an institution, a small community desperate to survive. It is, as the presiding bishop loves to remind us, a gathering of people who have

---

5. Joan Chittister, O.S.B, *The Rule of St. Benedict: Insights for the Ages* (New York: Crossroad Publishing, 1992), 27.

heard the call to follow Jesus in his way of love for the world, person by person, community by community.

The Seven Practices

The first practice in a Jesus-focused life is to *turn*—turn our gaze, our mind, our thoughts, our attention to Jesus. Simple as it sounds, it is the foundational practice, referring back to the first conscious decision we made, or have yet to make, to be a follower of Jesus. To turn also describes the daily decision to focus our attention on Jesus, asking for his guidance and grace.

The second practice is to *learn*, to commit each day to some form of learning, reading the Bible, or listening to devotional material focused on Jesus's teachings. Sometimes the learning process involves deep engagement through a class or study; other times, it's a small, daily encounter with sources of wisdom and inspiration. What matters most here isn't the quantity of our learning, but the steady commitment to take in a bit of insight each day.

The third practice, to *pray*, flows naturally from the first and second, yet also stands alone. We pray at all times and places. I have realized that sitting down in the same place every day for even a few minutes has a quiet, yet powerful impact on my life. It's a time to sort through and settle my thoughts, as murky water settles in stillness and allow bits of clarity to emerge. It's a time to speak my heart, often with sighs instead of words, before God. And it's a time to listen. We may not hear anything in the silence, but we might. And we never will hear anything from God if we don't take time to listen.

In terms of time, we can commit ourselves to *turn*, *learn*, and *pray* each day in as little as fifteen minutes a day. We can always spend more time, but the benefit comes with the habit of setting aside time, no matter the amount. It's best to start small.

The fourth practice, to *worship*, moves us from the personal to the collective. Following Jesus is a communal endeavor and we cannot grow in the ways of love on our own. We are nourished in faith through worship as we pray and sing together and open ourselves to the mysteries of sacrament. Theologian Norman Wirzba writes, "The church at its best is like a school that trains people in the way of love, an unusual school that lasts a lifetime and from which we never really graduate."[6] We apprentice ourselves to one another in Christian community and together experience Christ's presence.

The fifth practice, to *bless*, takes us out of our lives and churches and into the world around us. To bless, that is, to speak words of kindness and affirmation, is perhaps the loveliest and most understated of spiritual practices. Celtic author and poet John O'Donohue describes blessing as a lost art form. "The world can be harsh and negative," he writes, "but if we remain generous and patient, kindness inevitably reveals itself. Something deep in the human soul seems to depend on the presence of kindness; something instinctive in us expects it, and once we sense it, we are able to trust and open ourselves."[7] Each day we are given countless opportunities to speak kindness into another person's life, to offer a word of hope in times of uncertainty.

The sixth practice, to *go*, is for many the most challenging. This is the call to cross the borders of our familiarity in order to better understand the experience of another. The great criminal justice reformer of our time, Bryan Stevenson, speaks of being proximate to suffering, getting close to those who bear the brunt of our society's ills and coming to know them as neighbors and friends.[8]

---

6. Norman Wirzba, *Way of Love: Recovering the Heart of Christianity* (New York: HarperCollins, 2016), 8.

7. John O'Donohue, *To Bless the Space Between Us: A Book of Blessings* (New York: Doubleday, 2008), 185.

8. Bryan Stevenson, *Just Mercy: A Story of Justice and Redemption* (New York: Spiegel & Grau, 2014), 14.

Walking in the way of love requires us to show up in those places where love is needed most.

The final practice, to *rest*, is also one many struggle with and may well be the most countercultural for our time. Yet we are mortal, and our souls and bodies are restored in rest. To rest is to remember that we are not alone and that not everything depends on us. We can lay our burdens down and make space in our lives for renewal and the things that make for joy. Scripture teaches that sabbath isn't something we earn; it is our birthright as children of God.

Seven may seem like a daunting number of spiritual practices, and it would be if the goal was to check them off each day as tasks on our spiritual to-do list. I have found it helpful to ponder the seven practices over the course of a week, a month, and even a season of my life. We may be drawn, for our soul's sake, to a season of learning; we may feel an internal nudge to go beyond ourselves in some small or significant way. At the outset, you might ask: Which of the seven practices come easily for you? With which do you struggle? Is there one that speaks with particular urgency, as something your life needs right now?

The purpose of these intentional practices is to open ourselves to experience Jesus with us. So often we think of the Christian faith as an obligation, or as a set of beliefs that we must hold. There are obligations and beliefs, but if we get stuck there, we can lose sight of—or never experience at all—what is most important: Jesus's invitation to experience a loving, personal relationship with God. No matter our struggles and doubts, no matter our past sins or persistent failings, our relationship with God is one we can trust. In God we can find refuge and solid ground upon which to stand.

The Way of Love is the journey of a lifetime. It's a way of knowing God, receiving and sharing Jesus's love, and being a blessing to the world. As you read the reflections that follow, may you experience something of God's light and love for you.

To Turn

PAUSE, LISTEN, AND CHOOSE TO FOLLOW JESUS

Jesus said to Simon, "Do not be afraid; from now on you will be catching people." When they had brought their boats to shore, they left everything and followed him. —Luke 5:10–11

FOCUSING OUR LIFE ON JESUS begins with a turn. When someone calls us we turn our gaze. We turn our attention. Sometimes we turn around and go in a different direction. Whenever and however we turn, it is important to remember that we do so in response to a call, an awareness of someone or something beckoning within or outside us. While turning is our first step toward an encounter with God, we do not initiate the relationship. A relationship with God—and for Christians, a relationship with Jesus—never begins from our side. It always begins with God.

Our relationship with God begins much like the relationship we have as infants to our parents and other nurturing adults. Our parental images for God are embedded in the human psyche precisely because of our early experiences. Those who love us as infants do so for a long time before we even know what love is, much less love them in return. We must grow in our awareness of their love, our understanding of love, and our capacity to love before we can respond. In a lifelong process of growth, we learn, and continue to learn, what human love is.

Similarly, God loves us long before we are conscious of divine love. We can live for years, even a lifetime, unaware of God's love. Tragically, many people are deprived of human love to such a degree that the idea of a loving God seems inconceivable and even offensive. Yet it is also true that awareness of God requires an openness on our part, a willingness to suspend judgment or activity long enough to notice what is asking for our attention.

The essential message of the gospel, suggests former archbishop of Canterbury Rowan Williams, is that God is more interested in us than we are in God. He writes, "The good news is that if we show signs of response, of trust and love, then that interest turns into profound intimacy and relationship."[1] It's not surprising that many of us have significant spiritual experiences during times of great vulnerability or joy, for those are the times when we often let our guard down. In vulnerability we can be more receptive to the mysterious presence and loving presence of God.

Like responding to a hand extended to join someone on the dance floor, only we can decide to turn toward our experience of a spiritual encounter. In the early stages of our conscious relationship with God, or a return to an intentional relationship, our first steps are nonetheless in response to an invitation that comes to us from God.

There are numerous stories in the biblical accounts of Jesus's life that illustrate this relational dynamic of encounter and response. They are part of a larger biblical genre known as "call stories," for in them key biblical characters hear God or Jesus call and they must choose whether or not to respond. We might also refer to them as "invitation stories" because in an encounter or experience, an invitation is extended, and Jesus awaits our response.

---

1. Rowan Williams, "God's Mission and Ours in the 21st Century," ICS Lecture at Lambeth Palace, London, June 9, 2009.

One of my favorite invitation stories in the Bible takes place early in Jesus's public ministry. As the story is told in the Gospel according to Luke, Jesus was teaching and healing throughout the small villages in northern Israel near a lake known as the Sea of Galilee. The response by the people living in this area to Jesus was immediate and enthusiastic, such that crowds began to follow him wherever he went.

One day, Jesus asked two fishermen if he could use one of their boats as a speaking platform from the water, in order that he might speak to those gathered on the shore. Though they had just returned from a long and unsuccessful night of fishing, one of the fishermen, named Simon, agreed to row Jesus out onto the water. When Jesus finished teaching, he turned to Simon and said, "Put out into the deep water and let down your nets for a catch." That's when readers of the story realize that Jesus's primary objective wasn't to teach the crowd, but to spend time alone with Simon. Simon gently reminded Jesus that he and his partners had been out all night and caught nothing. No doubt he was exhausted and convinced from his futile efforts that there was no use in lowering his nets again. Nonetheless, Simon agreed: "If you say so," he said, "I'll let down the nets."

In his book *Simon Peter: Flawed but Faithful Disciple*, Adam Hamilton suggests that "yet if you say so," is an expression of Simon's "reluctant obedience," something to which we can all relate. "There are times," Hamilton writes, "when Jesus asks us to do things that we don't want to do, when we're tired, or when what we're being asked makes no sense to us. . . . For us, the deep water is the place where Jesus calls us to go when we'd rather stay on the shore."[2]

I can hear the tone of reluctant obedience in Peter's response. I can also imagine Peter saying "if you say so," with the kind of

---

2. Adam Hamilton, *Simon Peter: Flawed but Faithful Disciple* (Nashville: Abingdon, 2018). Kindle Edition, 372–375.

exasperation meant to convey, "You clearly don't know what you're talking about, but to humor you and even to prove you wrong, I'll do what you say." In my more wistful moments, I hear Simon speaking from a place of weary hopefulness. He was willing to cast his net one more time in case a few fish might show up to redeem his failed efforts thus far.

With whatever meaning Simon said what he said, what matters is that Simon did what Jesus asked him to do. Within minutes, there were more fish to catch than his nets could hold. In a pivotal turning point for Simon, he fell to his knees overwhelmed with shame. "Go away from me, Lord," he said, "for I am a sinful man." Clearly this wasn't shame for having doubted Jesus's fishing sensibilities. Simon suddenly recognized Jesus in a new way; he realized that he was in the presence of someone holy, and he didn't feel worthy. Surely if Jesus knew what kind of man he was, Jesus wouldn't want anything to do with him.

But Jesus did know him. He knew all about him. He didn't ask Simon for help because he wanted Simon's boat. He wanted Simon. "Follow me," he said. "From now on, you and I will be fishing for people." Simon turned to follow Jesus and his life would be forever changed (Luke 5:1–11).

What I love about Simon's encounter with Jesus is that it describes so beautifully how Jesus shows up in our lives and makes his presence known before he asks us to follow him. Obviously, we won't experience Jesus as Simon and others did when Jesus walked the earth. Jesus comes to us now in spirit. He comes in and through other people. He speaks through our thoughts and dreams, through the events in our lives, through what we read, listen to, or watch. When we see Jesus now, we see him with our inner eye. When we hear him, we hear him in our heart. Our relationship with Jesus begins not with us, but with him coming to us. Only then is the invitation extended for us to turn toward him who has first turned toward us.

A Life of Turning

I know many Christians who cannot remember the first time they consciously turned toward Jesus. "Jesus has always been with me," they say, with no memory of it being otherwise. "I met Jesus at the kitchen table," writes Rachel Held Evans in *Inspired*, published the year before her tragic death:

> It was at that table, over a steaming plate of spaghetti or pork chops or some other weekday meal that I learned to pray, "Jesus, thank you for Mommy and Daddy and Rachel and Amanda, and thank you for this food. Amen." The first thing I knew about Jesus was that he was responsible for the existence of my parents, my sister, me, and my food. That seemed like good enough news for me.[3]

For others of us, the encounter was more dramatic. Words seem inadequate when we attempt to talk about such encounters—what we sometimes call our conversion experience. But in essence what we're trying to describe is our experience of invitation and response, of turning toward the one who first turned toward us.

I am among those who vividly remembers the first time I consciously turned toward Jesus. It happened in my early adolescence when I was living in somewhat of a religious vacuum. As a young child I had gone to church with my mother. But when I was eleven, I moved to live with my father and stepmother. We didn't attend church, and I can't remember God ever being the subject of conversation. Thus everything I thought I knew about God and Jesus in those formative years was either picked up from television, seen in the movie "The Exorcist" (which came out when I was thirteen), or was what little I remembered from attending Sunday School when I was younger.

---

3. Rachel Held Evans, *Inspired: Slaying Giants, Walking on Water, and Loving the Bible Again* (Nashville: Nelson Books, 2018), Kindle Version, 147.

In ninth grade I became friends with a girl named Kelly. With an ease that astonished me, Kelly spoke freely about her Christian faith. I suppose if someone had asked me if I were a Christian, I would have said yes, because there were no other plausible options. But Kelly's self-description was different. It was personal and warm. Kelly spoke of Jesus as if she knew him, and that knowing him was a wonderful thing.

One Sunday, Kelly and her family invited me to join them for church, and I accepted. That day the minister spoke at length about Jesus's love, using the image of a door. "There's a door to our heart," he said. "Jesus waits outside for us to invite him in." I wasn't sure what he meant, but I knew that my heart was a lonely place. If Jesus wanted to come in, I was ready. Not even knowing it existed before that moment, I longed for the kind of love the minister was describing.

When the minister invited those who wanted to invite Jesus into their hearts to come forward, I somehow made my way to the front. He gently put his hands on my head, and he prayed. I don't remember what he said and I didn't feel all that different when I returned to my seat. But something changed for me that day. I had turned toward Jesus.

This was not a happy time in my life and inviting Jesus into my heart didn't make things better. My father and stepmother were struggling financially and in their marriage. My dad spent most evenings drinking bourbon and watching television. The social scene at school was also pretty miserable for me during those years. I felt that there was something wrong with me, that I didn't measure up, that I wasn't worthy of love. Because I was still struggling in so many ways, I wondered if I missed something in my conversion experience, or if somehow, I went about it in the wrong way.

In contrast, Kelly and her family were overjoyed about my decision to accept Jesus as my Savior. I wanted to be as happy as they were, but I wasn't. I don't remember ever doubting Jesus, but I was fairly sure that my conversion hadn't gone as far as it was meant to.

I even wondered aloud if I should go forward to receive the minister's prayer again. No one else thought that was a good idea.

As time went on, Kelly and I drifted apart and I stopped attending her church. I made other friends who were Christians, and with them I started attending a Young Life group at our high school. I sang in a number of high school choirs, and the choir director was a kind, Christian man. He looked out for me whenever he could.

Looking back, I realize now that there were all sorts of people looking out for me, and most of them were Christians.

One day a local minister showed up in our choir class and invited any who were interested to join their church choir on a singing tour to Mexico. Mexico! My friends and I jumped at the chance, and we soon found ourselves enveloped by another church community, one that was also on the "altar call/accept Jesus into your heart" end of the Christian spectrum. I became close friends with the minister's daughter and harbored a secret crush on her older brother who directed the choir.

When the time came, we traveled by bus and sang our hearts out for Jesus in small churches in southern Colorado and through New Mexico to the Texas/ Mexico border towns of El Paso and Juarez. In Juarez, I felt the incongruence of singing about Jesus's love in a church with a dirt floor, among people so poor that their children had no shoes. We never discussed their poverty as we prepared to sing—our goal was to help them accept Jesus as their Savior. As we were leaving, a young girl took my hand. We walked outside together, and there she gave me a bracelet. I was overwhelmed by her generosity and made a pledge in my heart to return someday to Juarez, to make a difference in her life. I never saw her again, but through that encounter something shifted in me. It was another turn.

When we came back to Colorado, the minister, who could tell that I was struggling on many levels, suggested that I be baptized. My infant baptism meant nothing, he said, for I was too young to make a personal commitment to follow Jesus. I agreed, hoping that finally I might have a proper conversion experience and know for myself the joy and peace we sang about in choir. So one Sunday afternoon I was baptized in the swimming pool of the minister's apartment complex. I'm not sure that it changed much except my standing in that church. When my father and stepmother's marriage ended, I lived for a time with the minister of that church and his family. I was all in.

Gradually, though, my identity as a Christian took hold. I leaned on and learned from more seasoned Christians. I felt the sustaining power of a loving Christian community as my family life collapsed. I had good friends. I still struggled inside with some of the church's more rigid beliefs. I simply couldn't reconcile Jesus's love with the notion that only a narrow few—those who believed exactly the way we did—would be saved. I longed for a place to talk about my struggles, but trying to do so only seemed to make others uncomfortable around me. I wanted to talk about the gap between what we prayed on Sunday mornings and how we actually lived our lives. But there wasn't room for that either. There was no place for ambiguity or doubt, and I was feeling a lot of both.

Of one thing I grew increasingly clear: it was time to return to live with my mother. I didn't want to leave my friends, but I knew, in a way that I had never known anything as clearly, that I had to go. The minister and his wife agreed that I needed to be with family, but they worried I would "backslide" if I didn't find another "believers' church." I already knew that I wasn't going to look for that kind of church. But it wasn't Jesus I was rejecting. In fact, I felt closer to Jesus than I had ever before. Leaving Colorado on my own was both terrifying and heartbreaking, the hardest decision of my young life, but I didn't feel alone. I felt Jesus with me, and gratefully, I turned toward him.

Sometimes I wonder if I would have remained a Christian if I had stayed in Colorado. As thankful as I am to communities that introduced me to Jesus and welcomed me into their fold, I'm not sure how much longer I would have lasted within the confines of their non-negotiable beliefs. But as grace would have it, returning to live with my mother also brought me back to the Episcopal congregation I had attended as a child and where my mother was now an active lay leader.

I owe my lifelong faith and vocation to Christ Episcopal Church, which was then located in Stanhope, New Jersey, and to the minister, the Rev. Richard Constantinos, who took me under his wing and helped me work through my endless questions. When I told him that I didn't believe that only a very narrow group of Christians would be saved, whatever being saved meant, he agreed with me. "A good rule of thumb when thinking about God," he said, "is to assume if you wouldn't do something because it isn't loving or kind, then God—who is the source of all love—wouldn't do it either." That insight changed my life, and it remains foundational for me. Presiding Bishop Curry likes to say something similar: "If it's not about love, it's not about God." I felt another turn toward a broader understanding of Jesus and what it meant to follow him.

A few years later, the horizons of my faith expanded yet again when I was introduced to Christians whose faith propelled them into the work of social justice. This was during the Central American wars of the 1980s, when men and women of faith were dying for their commitment to stand with the poor. I was in college, among Christians who were actively fighting for a change in our foreign policy, and I felt the rightness of our cause. Yet other Christians were supporting that foreign policy, in the name of anticommunism. In college I also first met gays and lesbians who were fighting for the right to be themselves and be fully accepted in society. Some of the most articulate and outspoken gay and lesbian activists I met were Christians, even as other Christians pushed back with an interpretation of scripture that condemned what they called "the homosexual lifestyle."

And it was in those formative college years that I first studied the life and writings of the Rev. Martin Luther King Jr. As I read everything I could get my hands on about the Civil Rights struggle that I had been oblivious to as a young child in the 1960s, I saw again how there were Christians on both sides of the great struggle for racial justice. Many of the ones whom I knew in my heart to be on the wrong side were the very people who had introduced me to Jesus. Even my beloved Episcopal priest, who had become a surrogate father figure in my life, disapproved of the direction my life was taking.

This was yet another turning, this time toward a social justice expression of Jesus's gospel. I now worshipped with socially minded Roman Catholics and Quakers. My first job after college was with a Methodist social service agency in Tucson, Arizona, where we tried to help economic refugees from the Rust Belt and Central American refugees seeking political asylum in Canada. While I was the only person in my work and social circles with an affiliation with the Episcopal Church, I could never bring myself to leave it. I found an Episcopal Church in Tucson and worshipped there. When asked why, the only explanation I could give was, "It feels like home."

I share my experience here to illustrate how turning toward Jesus isn't something we do once and are done with; rather, turning is part of our journey through life that changes and grows as we change and grow. The first time I came forward in a church to accept Jesus as my Savior and Lord was the first conscious turning point, but there have been many others, some more dramatic than others. At any point along the way, I could have decided to turn away, or drift away from the path of following Jesus, as many have done. But I can't say that it was ever something I seriously considered.

There's a story in the Gospel according to John that tells of a time when many of Jesus's disciples turned back from following him after he had preached a particularly challenging message. Jesus then turned to his closest disciples, the twelve who had been with him from the beginning. "Do you also wish to go away?" Simon

Peter responded, "Lord, to whom would we go? You have the words of eternal life. We have come to believe and know that you are the Holy One of God" (John 6:66–69). Clearly, they had journeyed too far with Jesus to turn back now.

I have responded in much the same way at pivotal junctures in my life. Whatever the challenge, whatever new insights or experiences I am given, however the church and those who profess to follow Jesus betray his essential teachings, I never felt there was another path for me. Nor, however, have I felt compelled to judge those who do not feel called to the Christian life. For faith to be authentic, it must be freely chosen, not out of fear or coercion, but in response to compelling love.

In a similar way, once I returned to the Episcopal Church in high school, I never seriously considered leaving it, although I worshipped freely and often in other traditions and was encouraged to pursue ordination in two of them. It's not that I have seen the Episcopal Church through rose-colored glasses. Throughout my life, I have been painfully aware of our institutional weaknesses, and I am often embarrassed and frustrated by them. Still my love for the Episcopal Church and sense of being at home within it goes deeper than I can articulate. I can point to many factors: the mystical connection to Christ in the Eucharist; the intellectual rigor and expansiveness of its theology; the courageous example of Episcopal leaders I have known. But in the end, what I say with confidence is that I simply feel called to follow Jesus in and through the Episcopal Church.

As my work with the Methodists was coming to an end, I mustered up the courage to officially enter the ordination process in the Episcopal Church. There was a strong bias in those years against younger adults seeking ordination. People like me, in our early twenties, were often told to seek secular employment for a few years before pursuing ordination. If that was the answer I received, my Methodist clergy friends assured me there was a place for me among their ranks. But I knew that I at least needed to try to serve in the church that felt like home.

I also needed to return to New Jersey, because the Diocese of Arizona was not yet open to the ordination of women. This meant seeking the blessing of Richard Constantinos, who had been such a formative influence in my life, and yet had never encouraged me whenever I spoke to him about ordination. As I traveled home, the image of knocking at a door kept coming back to me. My first turning toward Jesus involved opening the door of my heart to let him in. Now I was knocking on the door of the Episcopal Church, to see if I would be accepted as a potential priest. When I met with Constantinos, to my astonishment he said, "I was waiting for you to be clear within yourself." Then to the bishop. Then to the Commission on Ministry. Each door I knocked upon, to my amazement and eternal gratitude, opened before me.

As part of the ordination process, I was required to write a spiritual autobiography, which was a revelatory experience. Prior to that exercise of deep reflection, I had considered my life as a series of random, often chaotic, and unrelated episodes. But as I wrote, I realized that there was, in fact, a story to my life. In retrospect, I could see more clearly some of what I've attempted to describe here, the ways Jesus made his presence known to me, or guided me without my awareness, at pivotal moments.

It was also revelatory to recognize the vital role other Christians had on my life, those who embodied a living faith that I both admired and wanted to emulate. It's sometimes said that the Christian faith is caught, not taught, for it is the living examples of faith that most inspire, more than anything we might read in scripture. That was, and remains true, for me. Looking back, I could also see the importance of my response, that I had indeed turned toward him, and that Jesus, in turn, honored my best, imperfect intentions to follow him.

I also realized in ways that truly worried me how wounded and broken I felt inside. On the surface, I had the ability to convey a confidence that I rarely felt. Internally I was vulnerable and needy and carrying a heavy burden of shame. Fortunately for me, the ordination process included an in-depth psychological examination. Suffice it to say that I was terrified. Surely the psychologist would see all that I was doing to keep the worst of me at bay. In fact, I think he did. He pointed out what were, for me, devastating observations about my inner life. He gently and matter-of-factly told me that I had real work to do, and he urged me to find a therapist when I got to seminary. I looked straight into his eyes. "Did you just say '*when I got to seminary?*'" I could barely take it in: that despite all my flaws, he saw in me the makings of a priest.

I have come a long way from that first conscious step I took to turn toward Jesus within a strict fundamentalist Christian context, and also from my first steps toward ordained leadership in the Episcopal Church. The journey of daily turning and transformation of life continues. One of the many reasons I'm grateful to be part of the Episcopal Church is that every Sunday we are invited to come forward and invite Jesus into our hearts. Every week, he comes to us in the symbolic last supper. Every week, we can turn toward him and allow his spirit to fill us. Turning isn't meant to be a once-for-all experience but something we choose every day. As C. S. Lewis writes, "Relying on God has to begin all over again every day as if nothing had yet been done."[4]

Daily Turning

The Way of Love invites us to take a small step each day toward Jesus, reminding ourselves as we do, that he first turns toward us. It might be helpful for you, as it was for me, to consider the larger narrative of your life and the turning points in life and faith that you can more easily identify in retrospect. A daily practice of turning might feel like a rote exercise without the larger context of

---

4. W. H. Lewis, ed., *Letters of C. S. Lewis* (Orlando, FL: Harcourt, 1986), 220.

spiritual encounter and invitation that is at the heart of a relationship with Jesus. Like our spiritual forebears who took the time to write down their experiences of holy encounter so that they would not forget them and could then pass them down to others, we do well to remember those pivotal moments in the gospel of our lives. If you've never written a spiritual autobiography, you might start there. By remembering those holy moments and then adopting an intentional, daily practice of turning toward Jesus, we open ourselves both to experience his loving presence and to remind ourselves that his love is there for us even when we don't feel it.

When we choose to make turning toward Jesus a daily practice, the first thing we realize is that some days we're better at it than others. We aren't always very good at turning toward him. To state the obvious, turning requires practice. It's helpful to begin with an audit of our early morning routine. When we first rise from sleep, there are physical needs to tend to, so we generally make our way to the bathroom. We may go immediately then to the kitchen for food or coffee. If there are others to care for in the morning, we must do that. Most of us have morning chores. Some of us like to exercise in the morning. Where might a daily practice of turning fit in?

My suggestion is this: sometime after you wake up and before you check your phone, turn on another electronic device, or do anything else to engage the world around you, find some way to turn toward Jesus. Consciously turn your mind, your inward eye, toward him. This might involve saying a prayer as you get up, when you stretch, look in the mirror, or take a shower. It can be as simple as remembering that he is there.

Since consciously adopting the Way of Love as my rule of life, I try to turn toward Jesus every day as I rise. I don't always remember, but whenever I do, I stop, take a breath, thank him for the day, offer whatever I'm feeling or thinking, and ask for his guidance and strength. I've noticed that when I remember to begin each morning by turning toward him, should something or someone get my attention later in the day—even if it feels like an interruption—I have a better chance of noticing his presence in that encounter. At the end of the day, it's also helpful to reflect back on the day and ask, "Where was Jesus present? Where did I feel his presence, or miss him in the moment because I wasn't paying attention?"

The daily practice of turning is, by design, brief, and best supplemented by the next two practices in the Way of Love: to *learn* and to *pray*. Yet if a longer time of learning and intentional prayer is not possible, the small effort of turning our gaze toward Jesus, when practiced daily, has the effect of opening our hearts and minds to receive him, and to be available to him in love for others.

Turning as Repentance

There is yet another dimension of turning toward Jesus for us to remember, one that is at the heart of Jesus's central message of repentance: "The time is fulfilled and the Kingdom of God has come near; repent, and believe in the good news" (Mark 1:15). The word *repentance*, translated from the Greek *metanoia*, means to have a change of heart or mind. There is a strong association of remorse—that we turn from things we have done or said that we now regret—and a commitment to change course, literally to turn around and walk in another direction.

In church, we often talk about Jesus forgiving our sins. What that means, at least in part, is that when we know we've said or done something wrong, or we've made a mistake with serious consequences and we don't know how to set things right, we can turn to Jesus. When we ask, he will forgive us. More than that, he will help us make amends and start anew. He will walk with us every step of the way. To ask for forgiveness doesn't allow us to forget, or pretend that what was hurtful or wrong never happened. The gift of repentance is finding a way out of the pain, a way to make amends and release us from the burden of what we've done.

So, too, when life gets rough and it's not our fault and we need help, Jesus is one to whom we can turn. I wrote earlier of the time as a teenager when I was alone, scared, and needed help. Jesus was there with me. I felt his presence and his strength.

If you are going through hard times now, I pray that you might dare to believe that you can turn to Jesus. May you know that he is there for you, for those you love, and for the brokenhearted of this world. Jesus doesn't miraculously make what's hard go away; what Jesus gives is inner strength and courage. He moves through other people who show up and help us. As is often said, he can make a way out of no way.

There is an element of faith in turning toward Jesus, a willingness to trust what we cannot know for certain. Spiritual experiences of invitation and response are not easily explained or understood, and they are fleeting and ambiguous enough for us to have a plausible alibi of deniability should we decide that we don't want to turn toward Jesus. The world is full of enough distorted, unappealing, and unloving expressions of Christianity to convince anyone that the entire Christian message is a sham. But for those who have known an experience of encounter with Jesus and have taken steps toward him in response, the assurance of God's love can become, if we allow it, the defining narrative of our lives. Like Jesus's first disciples, we have come to believe and know that he is God-with-us; through him we have received grace upon grace. There is nowhere else we would choose to go, no other path we would rather take.

Turning is the first of seven practices in a Jesus-centered life. It is the starting point, when we first make the decision to turn toward the one who has come to us. He walks into our lives that way he walked into Simon's, somehow getting our attention, inviting us to turn and follow. It's not a choice we make once, but daily, to turn toward him and follow where he leads. We turn to the One who first turns to us in love.

2

⌇

To Learn

REFLECT ON SCRIPTURE EACH DAY, ESPECIALLY ON JESUS'S LIFE AND TEACHINGS

The kingdom of heaven is like treasure hidden in a field, which someone found and hid; then in his joy he goes and sells all that he has and buys that field. —Matthew 13:44

THE SECOND PRACTICE for a Jesus-centered life invites us to reflect daily on Holy Scripture, especially Jesus's life and teaching.

As a backdrop for exploring the fruits of such a practice, I'd like to approach the topic of learning about God and from God in the broadest of terms, for God is everywhere. Everywhere we go, everything that happens, every person we meet can be a means through which we grow in our knowledge and love of God. Periodically I meet with a Jesuit priest for spiritual counsel, and as I share with him the joys and challenges of my life, he'll ask, "What is God trying to teach you through these experiences?" Or, "How is God shaping your heart?"

To frame the many ways we can learn about God and from God, I turn to one of the most beautiful and comprehensive prayers in the Episcopal Church's Book of Common Prayer (page 836), simply entitled "A General Thanksgiving." This prayer is worth committing to memory, for it speaks of life's breadth and depth, how God is known to us through all of life, and as a result how we can live with gratitude, even in times of struggle. It begins:

> Accept, O Lord, our thanks and praise for all that you have done for us. We thank you for the splendor of the whole creation, for the beauty of this world, for the wonder of life, and for the mystery of love.

Every corner of creation speaks of God's wondrous power: "the vast expanse of interstellar space, the galaxies, the sun, the planets in their courses;"[1] the miracle of an infant's birth; the smell of fresh bread; the sound of someone singing; the sun rising and setting each day.

Creation is also stronger than we are, and we are more vulnerable against the elements than we realize until we come up against the full power of nature. The poet David Whyte spent several years as a young man on the Galapagos Islands off the coast of Ecuador. He writes of what it was like to be in a part of the world virtually untouched by the human species: "I had come to study nature in all its glory, yet a secret portion of me found the Galapagos in its raw form intensely frightening. Everywhere I went, I saw animals living and dying according to some other mercy than my human mind could stand."[2] Human beings seemed out of place there, as if our existence were irrelevant.

The late Irish poet John O'Donohue writes of our place in the vast expanse of creation, "Humans are new here. Above us the galaxies dance out towards infinity. Under our feet is ancient earth. We are beautifully molded from this clay."[3] That we exist at all is a miracle, that we're here and have evolved as a species, that we

---

1. Eucharistic Prayer C, Book of Common Prayer, 369–372.

2. David Whyte, *Crossing an Unknown Sea: Work as a Pilgrimage of Identity* (New York: Berkley, 2001), 33.

3. John O'Donohue, *Anam Cara: Spiritual Wisdom from the Celtic World* (Great Britain: Bantam, 1997), 15.

can think with our minds and feel with our emotions. We learn of God, in whom we live and move and have our being, as we live and breathe, as we pay attention to both our natural surroundings and the inner terrain of our souls.

Learn from Love

> We thank you for the blessing of family and friends, and for the loving care which surrounds us on every side.

We learn of love through the experience of being loved. There is no other way. People who are raised by loving, emotionally mature parents are blessed with a solid foundation from which to experience other loving relationships throughout life, including a loving relationship with God. Jesus himself addressed God in prayer as *Abba*, the most intimate, familial term for father in his language. Those raised with a severe deficit of human love understandably struggle to trust the love of God. While no human being loves perfectly, it is through the love of other people, albeit imperfect, that we learn something of God's perfect love.

"There is power in love," Presiding Bishop Curry preached at the royal wedding in May 2018:

> If you don't believe me, think of a time when you first fell in love. The whole world seemed to center around you and your beloved. Oh there's power in love. Not just in its romantic form, but any form, any shape of love. There's a certain sense in which when you are loved, when someone cares for you and you know it, when you love and you show it—it actually feels right.[4]

Human imperfection in love also creates in us a longing for love that is unbroken and unconditional. As we come to know and

---

4. Michael Curry, *The Power of Love* (New York: Random, 2018), 8.

trust the unconditional love of God, revealed to us in Jesus, we grow in our capacity to accept human failings in love, our own and that of others.

If what we experience in human relationship is not loving, that lack of love is not of God, even if it is communicated by someone speaking or acting in God's name. I feel this is a statement that bears repeating for so many have been wounded by harsh and prejudicial teachings in the name of God. If we experience any kind of abuse or unkindness from another person in the name of God, what we are experiencing is not of God, for God is love.

Joan Chittister tells of a pivotal moment in her childhood when one of her teachers said something quite unloving in the name of God. Growing up in the 1940s, Joan lived in a predominantly Catholic neighborhood and attended Catholic school. In those years the boundary separating Roman Catholic from Protestant Christians in many parts of the United States was strict and uncompromising. Many Protestants viewed Roman Catholics with suspicion, and many Catholics felt the same way toward Protestants.

Joan, however, was raised in what was considered a religious mixed marriage. Her mother was Catholic; her father was Protestant. Joan didn't give much thought to her parents' religious differences until one day at school when her teacher said something that horrified her. Joan rushed home to speak to her mother before her father came home from work. Her mother asked her what was on her mind.

> "Sister said that only Catholics go to heaven," I said softly. "Oh really?" my mother said, still working at the sink. "And what do you think, Joan?" I took a deep breath. "I think Sister is wrong," I said. "And why do you think Sister would say a thing that's wrong?" my mother pressed. "Because," I whispered slowly, "Sister doesn't know Daddy." Sister, in other words was missing some of the evidence. . . . She clearly did not know what I knew. I looked up tentatively. Mine was simply standing there, smiling at

me. To this day, I can still see her look, still feel the grain of her apron against my face. She shook the suds off her hands, pulled me up close against her warm, hard stomach, and said, "That's right, darling, that's right."[5]

We'd have a hard time finding a Roman Catholic today who believes that everyone who isn't Catholic is going to hell; nor do most Protestants believe such a fate awaits Catholics. Now herself a nun, Joan had been blessed as a young child with a love that surrounded her on every side and transcended the false division between Catholics and Protestants of that time. Love gave her courage to think for herself in the face of an authority figure telling her something she knew was wrong. Intuitively she knew that what was not of love was not of God.

Learn from Creativity

> We thank you for setting us at tasks that demand our best efforts, and for leading us to accomplishments that satisfy and delight us.

We learn something of God's creative energy when we are inspired in imaginative endeavors. I believe that we are most at home in the world when we discover, develop, and express our unique creativity. The work itself is as varied as we are. For some, our true work is our profession or trade. It could also be working in the garden, cleaning our home, caring for children, singing in the choir, serving at the altar at church. It could be through works of art or acts of compassion.

Often our most satisfying and delighting work isn't what pays the bills, though we derive satisfaction from work done well. The same can be said for daily chores, those tasks that simply need to be

---

5. Joan Chittister, *In Search of Belief* (Liguori, Missouri: Liguori Triumph, 1999), 12.

finished. The work that delights and satisfies is what causes us to give our best efforts no matter the cost, that best aligns us with the creative energy of God. In spiritual language, this work is our vocation, our calling, part of the reason we are here.

My husband Paul worked professionally for many years in a job that he did well. It gave him satisfaction and through his work he helped provide for our family. But the deeper vocation of his life lies elsewhere.

Paul loves to observe and study birds, a passion he learned as a boy from his father. He can identify thousands of bird species by sight and song. Throughout the years he worked and helped raise our sons, he found time—never enough from his perspective —to go off in search of birds. I came to recognize that look in his eyes as he broached the subject of a birding trip. He sometimes bribed our young sons with a stop at Dairy Queen if they came with him on an expedition. He stayed up late at night recording migration patterns, writing articles for ornithology journals, keeping his lists current.

Now that Paul is retired, he is free to pursue his passion for birds around the country and the world. When he's home, he spends hours cataloging photographs, writing articles and books about his travels, and preparing for the next trip. It isn't always easy to live with someone with such singular passion, but Paul's vocation is to obey Jesus's imperative: *look at the birds*. I marvel at his dedication. In this work that satisfies and delights him, he not only learns of God's creative genius, he shares in it.

Learn from Pain

> We thank you also for those disappointments and failures that lead us to acknowledge our dependence on you alone.

The General Thanksgiving now enters challenging terrain. How can we thank God in sorrow? What can we possibly learn of God when our hearts are broken, when tragedy strikes, or when we carry the weight of our failures? We can learn of God's compassion and forgiveness, often mediated through those who walk with us and release us from the shame we feel. We can learn that failure, while excruciatingly painful, does not tell the whole story about us.

I don't want to minimize the pain we experience in disappointment and failure and move too quickly to the good that, by God's grace and human perseverance, can come from them. For the pain can be devastating and the grief we feel can leave us paralyzed for a long time. I am among the many deeply grateful for the work of Dr. Brené Brown, whose books and TED talks have helped remove the stigma of failure. One book in particular, *Rising Strong*, has been a lifeline for me, for in it she describes the excruciating process of getting up after falling hard.

> Yes, there can be no learning, innovation, or creativity without failure. But failing is painful. It fuels the "shouldas and couldas" which means judgment and shame are often lying in wait. Yes I agree with Tennyson who wrote "Tis better to have loved and lost than never to have loved at all." But heartbreaks knock the wind out of you, and the feelings of loss and longing can make getting out of bed a monumental task. . . . Yes if we care enough and dare enough we will experience disappointment. But in those moments when disappointment is washing over us and we're desperately trying to get our hearts and heads around what is or is not going to be, the death of our expectations can be painful beyond measure.[6]

There, in the pain, God's mercies come to us, often mediated through the kindness of others or in the solace of prayer.

---

6. Brené Brown, *Rising Strong* (New York: Random House, 2015). Kindle Edition, Location 248, 255.

The words of an old hymn beautifully describe what God wants us to learn in the hardest of times:

> There's a wideness in God's mercy
> Like the wideness of the sea
> There's a kindness in God's justice
> That is more than liberty.
> There is no place where earth's sorrows
> Are more felt than up in heaven
> There is no place where earth's failings
> Have such kindly judgement given.[7]

God is there to forgive, restore and yes, to teach lessons when our hearts are broken, when we've lost our way, or when we've failed and must start again.

Learn from Jesus

> Above all we thank you for your Son Jesus Christ; for the truth of His word and the example of his life; for his steadfast obedience, by which he overcame temptation; for his dying through which he overcame death; and for his rising to life again, through which we are raised to the life of your kingdom.
>
> Grant us the gift of your Spirit, that we may know him and make him known, and through him, at all times and in all places may give thanks to you in all things.

The final two stanzas of this prayer of thanksgiving turn our gaze, at last, toward Jesus, describing him in ways that make us want to know him better. And where do we go to learn the truth of Jesus's

---

7. "There's a Wideness in God's Mercy," *The Hymnal 1982* (New York: Church Hymnal, 1982), hymn 469, 470.

word and the example of his life? To the biblical accounts of "the truth of his word and the example of his life."

This brings us to the second daily practice in the Way of Love: to *learn* of God, and in particular of Jesus's love, by reading and reflecting upon Jesus's life and teachings. We can learn about Jesus in many ways, and experience his loving presence through all manner of encounter. Yet there is no better way to know him and to grow in our relationship with him than to spend time each day reading and meditating on his life and teachings. In the gospel texts, we hear his voice and encounter him through the voices of those who knew him when he walked this earth, and of those whose lives were forever changed because of him. We begin to understand the reasons why those in his presence found themselves thinking, in the words of world religions scholar Huston Smith, "that if divine goodness were to manifest itself in human form, this is how it would behave."[8]

Because biblical texts are thousands of years old, written from a worldview far different from our own, we are wise to read with guidance and in the context of Christian community. We do well to pick our guides carefully, because it is possible to be not only confused by the Bible, but bullied with it and to have our intelligence insulted. Every prejudice known to humankind can be justified by something written somewhere in the Bible. Even Satan quoted scripture when Jesus faced temptation in the wilderness (Matt. 4:1–11). Still, there is so much to be gained by simply sitting down to read the gospel accounts of Jesus's life. You don't have to be a biblical scholar to feel the power of Jesus's presence reaching out to you as you read.

There are four accounts of Jesus's life, and each tells his story from a particular point of view. If you've never read any of the

---

8. Huston Smith, *The Soul of Christianity* (San Francisco: HarperSanFrancisco, 2005), 48.

gospels from start to finish, or if you've been away from scripture reading for a long time, you might try reading the gospels in what is widely believed to be the order in which they were written: the Gospels according to Mark, Matthew, Luke, and finally, John. The Gospel of John is the most complex, and Jesus sounds and acts quite differently there than in the first three. While John's gospel makes the case most directly, all four authors write from the conviction that Jesus is the One sent from God, that he was and is God, and that through him we might know the fullness of God's love.

Read with a spirit of openness and curiosity in the context of prayer. Take your time. If something troubles or confuses you, you can do one of two things: skip that part and keep going, or go deeper in your investigation. Don't take on too much at one time: a paragraph or two, maybe a story—no more than a chapter a day. If you'd like further guidance or suggesions for your learning, there are many fine tools and resources readily available. You can find a good selection on the Episcopal Church's website.[9] If you already have a daily practice of scripture reading or are part of a group Bible study, I hope my words here simply encourage you in your practice.

Loaves and Fish

In the Gospel of John, Jesus tells a leader of the Pharisees named Nicodemus, who came to him by night, that we must speak of what we know and testify to what we have seen (John 3:11). It is through a regular practice of scripture reading that we learn what Nicodemus saw with his own eyes—of what to speak and testify. I close this chapter with a bit of personal testimony, one example of God transforming my life through a particular story from the gospels.

When I began life as an ordained priest, I was also a new parent. As any new parent can attest, life was full and complicated. I

---

9. *https://www.episcopalchurch.org/way-of-love/practice/learn.*

wasn't getting much sleep, and I often felt that I was in the wrong place. When I was at work, I missed being with our son; when I was with him, I worried about not being fully present at work.

I came to ordained ministry with a strong desire to be active and engaged in the wider community of Toledo, Ohio, where we were living at the time. But in those early years, I wondered how I would ever find the time and energy for anything except working at the church and caring for our son. Then I received an invitation to serve on an advisory board for the local food bank that served as a distribution center for all the meal programs and food pantries in the city. I jumped at the opportunity, for it would allow me to fulfill the desire to be of service to those in need without making a huge time commitment.

Suffice to say that it didn't take long before I felt like a total failure in this modest endeavor. I managed to make it to the monthly meetings, but I didn't do any of the other things expected from board members, such as raise money, visit food sites, speak in the wider community on behalf of the poor. All I did was show up at the meetings, and as the months went by I felt increasingly inadequate. I half expected to be asked to step down so that a more engaged person would take my seat. But that never happened, and I chose to stick things out for the two-year term.

As I was driving to my last meeting, I prepared a short speech of apology for my lack of engagement. Before I could open my mouth, the head of the board gave a speech of her own, profusely thanking me for my service and listing all the ways that I had made significant contributions to this ministry. She lifted me up as an example of rising leadership in the city, and the whole board applauded! I was stunned. How on earth to make sense of the praise that the board president showered on me? Her words didn't change my internal assessment of my meager contribution, but I also didn't get the sense that she was embellishing the truth to make me feel better.

The next morning, as I sat in my prayer chair and read from one of the gospel accounts of Jesus's life, I came to the story sometimes referred to as the miracle of the loaves and fish. It tells of a time when Jesus had been teaching an entire day before a large crowd. As the sun began to set, Jesus's disciples approached him and said, "Master, it's late, and there's no food for all these people. Tell them to go home." Jesus replied, "You give them something to eat." "You can't be serious," they essentially replied. "We don't have enough food even to feed a few people." Jesus then asked them what they had. In one version of this story, the disciples produced a few loaves and some fish. In another version, a young boy came forward to offer what bread and fish he had. However they came to him, Jesus took the loaves and fish, offered them to God in thanksgiving and blessing, and then instructed the disciples to distribute the food among the people. There was more than enough food to feed the multitudes, with baskets left over (Matt. 14:13–21; John 6:1–13).

As I read, tears welled in my eyes. I realized that I had experienced a loaves-and-fish miracle of my own. My service on the advisory board was clearly not enough to meet the needs before me. Yet, by God's grace, what others experienced was something far greater than my meager offering. As clearly as I have ever heard anything from God, I heard and understood that what Jesus needed from me was to make my offering, no matter how insufficient it seemed to me. Then it was in his hands to do what only he can do.

The miracle of the loaves and fish remains the most important story in my spiritual narrative. Nearly every day I am faced with a need that I cannot meet and tasks I cannot accomplish. Nearly every day, I think of the loaves and fish and make my offering anyway. I don't understand how the miracle of abundance works; I only know that, on occasion, it does.

Sitting in my prayer chair that morning nearly thirty years ago, I wasn't simply reading a story about Jesus; the story was, in a sense, reading me. It gave me a powerful spiritual metaphor with which to interpret my life and better understand how God chooses to work with us for purposes beyond our knowing.

I've had similar experiences with other stories and teachings from scripture, more than I can count. It doesn't happen every time I sit down to read, but it happens often enough for me to anticipate and expect God to speak into my life through the stories and teachings from Jesus's life.

As an ordained person, I have also devoted many hours to studying the Bible in depth and I know the spiritual value of a strong foundation of biblical knowledge. By way of comparison, I think of my husband's knowledge of birds. When he sees a bird, he has a vast knowledge base with which to interpret the moment; seeing a particular bird means a lot more to him than it does to me. I see a bird whose characteristics I won't remember, because I have no internal scaffolding on which to place it. So it is, too, with the Bible. The more you know about the specific texts and their contexts, the more helpful they can be, and the easier it is to assess their spiritual significance. There are many resources for in-depth learning which I commend to you when your life affords time for such study. It's also a wonderful experience to read scripture in community with other people, drawing from their insights, questions, and experiences. Your daily practice of learning will be the richer for it.

Yet there is great spiritual value, no matter your level of biblical knowledge, in simply reading small portions of the gospels each day. Hear Jesus speak. Watch how he interacts with people. See how people respond to his message, his way of love. Take note of the questions he asks: "What do you want me to do for you?" "Which one of these was the neighbor to the man in need?" "Who do you say that I am?" Feel the power of his personal connection to God, whom he calls Father in the most familiar of terms and encourages us to do the same. Read a given text, and then let the text read you. Let it give insight and guidance and strength for your life, so that you may live every day giving thanks to God for the entirety of your life, through which God also speaks. There is so much for us to learn.

> Accept, O Lord, our thanks and praise for all that you have done for us. We thank you for the splendor of the whole creation, for the beauty of this world, for the wonder of life, and for the mystery of love.
>
> We thank you for the blessing of family and friends, and for the loving care which surrounds us on every side.
>
> We thank you for setting us at tasks that demand our best efforts, and for leading us to accomplishments that satisfy and delight us.
>
> We thank you also for those disappointments and failures that lead us to acknowledge our dependence on you alone.
>
> Above all we thank you for your Son Jesus Christ; for the truth of His word and the example of his life; for his steadfast obedience, by which he overcame temptation; for his dying through which he overcame death; and for his rising to life again, through which we are raised to the life of your kingdom. Grant us the gift of your Spirit, that we may know him and make him known, and through him, at all times and in all places may give thanks to you in all things. Amen.

3

~⁑~

To Pray

TO DWELL INTENTIONALLY
WITH GOD EACH DAY

He was praying in a certain place, and after he had finished, one of his disciples said to him, "Lord, teach us to
pray, as John taught his disciples." —Luke 11:1

ON A SCALE OF ONE TO TEN, I wonder how would you rate
the quality of your personal prayer life. For many, and I often find
myself among them, the thought of prayer evokes feelings of inad-
equacy, doubt, even skepticism. What are we doing when we pray?
Are we asking God to intervene for us in ways that God would not
otherwise? Why would God answer the prayers of some but not all?
Is there a right way, and conversely, a wrong way to pray?

For some the practice of prayer comes easily or is a well-estab-
lished spiritual practice. Yet the majority of people I speak with,
including clergy, find prayer to be a source of anxiety. If you reg-
ularly attend church, it can be hard to acknowledge how anemic
your personal prayers can be. If you've walked into a church for the
first time and hear others reciting strange and beautiful words, it
can feel as if you're the only one wondering what the words mean
and what difference it makes to say them. Rest assured that you are
not alone.

If you were to ask me to rate my life of prayer, I would say that it depends on the day. There are some days when I feel close to God in prayer and other days when I don't. I deeply value the practice of private prayer yet don't always make time for it. I've been a Christian leader for over half of my life, and still there are times when I feel like I'm starting over in prayer. But perhaps "a beginner's mind," as the Buddhists say, and a posture of humility, is a good place to start—or start again—in prayer.

Those who have devoted their lives to helping others to pray go to great lengths to assure the rest of us that prayer is as natural for human beings as breathing. As one example, monk and author Martin Laird writes:

> Communion with God in the silence of the heart is a God-given capacity, like the rhododendron's capacity to flower, the fledgling's for flight, and the child's for self-forgetful abandon and joy. If the grace of God that suffuses and simplifies the vital generosity of our lives does not consummate this capacity while we live; the very arms of God that embrace us as we enter the transforming mystery of death will surely do so.[1]

I found Laird's words especially consoling as I sat at my father's side in his final hours of life. While not a man of prayer or faith, near the end he had what looked to me to be a mystical encounter. He looked up from his hospital bed as if seeing something wondrously beautiful come toward him, his whole body straining to rise and meet what he alone saw. Then he gently rested back on his pillow. A few hours later he was gone. I hope for a similar experience when my time comes.

For me, prayer often begins with a request: please help. The good news is that there is help to be had, and gracious exhortations

---

1. Martin Laird, *Into the Silent Land: A Guide to the Christian Practice of Contemplation* (New York: Oxford University Press, 2006), 1.

for us to be of good courage when we pray. "There's something to be said in keeping prayer simple," writes Anne Lamott in her book on prayer, *Help, Thanks, Wow*.[2]

Struggles in prayer notwithstanding, I have learned that it is possible to become more confident in our relationship with God. Through the practice of prayer, we can learn to avail ourselves of the divine source of strength that is the presence of God in our lives. Through prayer, we can know ourselves to be unconditionally loved and find guidance as we strive to live meaningful lives. It is helpful to remember that God wants us to experience prayer, not as a weighty obligation, but rather a source of refreshment and clarity, where we can know ourselves to be forgiven and loved. It's also where we can hand over the reins of our lives to God, praying as Jesus prayed on the Mount of Olives, "Your will, not mine, be done" (Luke 22:42 paraphrased).

But what is prayer, exactly? The dictionary definition is "a solemn request for help or expression of thanks addressed to God or other object of worship." The Book of Common Prayer defines prayer as "responding to God, by thought and by deeds, with or without words," a lovely reminder that God initiates and we respond.[3] A beloved saint of the Roman Catholic Church, Thérèse of Lisieux, wrote this: "For me, prayer is an aspiration of the heart, a simple glance directed to heaven. It is a cry of gratitude and love in the midst of trial as well as joy."

I gravitate toward the straightforward definition of prayer as simply conversation with God. Sometimes we're aware of the conversation and sometimes we're not, for we pray most naturally when we aren't conscious of what we're doing—when we close our eyes, stare off into the distance, or get lost in our thoughts. We pray in

---

2. Anne Lamott, *Help, Thanks, Wow: The Three Essential Prayers* (New York: Riverhead Books, 2012), 1.

3. Book of Common Prayer, 856.

that luminous space at the edge of the day, as we're waking up in the morning and falling asleep at night. We pray when we feel most vulnerable. Of vulnerability in prayer Paul writes, "Likewise the Spirit helps us in our weakness; for we do not know how to pray as we ought, but that very Spirit intercedes with sighs too deep for words. And God, who searches the heart, knows what is the mind of the Spirit, because the Spirit intercedes for the saints according to the will of God" (Rom. 8:26–27). It's comforting to realize that the Spirit of God within us is helping our spirit to pray; humbling, too, that God searches and knows our hearts, as the beginning of one of our Sunday morning prayers reminds us: "O God to whom all hearts are open, all desires known, and from whom no secrets are hid."[4]

We also pray when we gather in church and say beautiful words that others have crafted. This can be a powerful experience, evoking deep emotions and a sense of connection to something beyond ourselves. We can lean on another's faith when ours seems distant. But reciting prayers can also feel rote and meaningless, and the beauty of poetically crafted words can make us feel inadequate about our far less elegant words of prayer.

With or without Words

It's said that if you want to make Episcopalians anxious, ask us to pray without a book. Years ago, members of the congregation I served had purchased a new home and they asked me to offer a house blessing. There are lovely house blessing prayers in one of the Episcopal Church's many prayer books, and I was happy to go to their house and offer those prayers. But when I arrived, I realized that I had forgotten the book. Panicked, I turned back to church for my forgotten prayer book. As I drove, I thought to myself, "Well, this is embarrassing. You can't come up with a house blessing

---

4. Book of Common Prayer, 355.

of your own?" After that, I resolved to practice and become more comfortable praying out loud without a text.

Of course, we pray with more than our words. We pray through artistic expression, such as music. As Augustine famously said, "Those who sing pray twice." We pray with our actions. The twentieth-century rabbi Abraham Joshua Heschel was among the many people of faith who answered Dr. Martin Luther King Jr.'s call to the join the civil rights march from Selma to Montgomery, Alabama, in 1965. Of that experience he later said, "I felt as if I was praying with my feet." I, too, feel as if I'm praying when absorbed in an endeavor that involves creativity or sacrificial love.

There are countless ways we are in conversation with God, not necessarily involving direct speech. But let's focus now on the form of prayer that is actual conversation with God, for it is here, I believe, that our daily intention and practice matter most.

As with any relationship, our relationship with Christ moves to greater depths of intimacy and trust when we tend to that relationship. The Quaker author Richard Foster aptly describes this daily practice of conversation with God, "Simple Prayer,"[5] for its requirements are not difficult. Little more is needed than our willingness to show up. With practice, it's easier to trust that Jesus shows up, too. In the words of Anne Lamott, "Prayer means that, in some unique way, we believe we're invited into a relationship with someone who hears us when we speak in silence."[6]

Daily Prayer

If you already have an established practice of daily prayer, may what follows serve as affirmation and encouragement in your practice. If

---

5. Richard J. Foster, *Prayer: Finding the Heart's True Home* (New York: Harper Collins, 1992), 7.

6. Lamott, 4.

you don't have such a practice, I urge you to try. If you're like me and periodically realize that weeks have gone by without my taking time to sit down to pray, don't be afraid to begin again.

Making time for daily prayer is worth the effort, for it has the power to change the course of your life for the better. Daily prayer can guide you through the most perplexing times, sustain you with strength when you need it most, validate your gifts and encourage you to take them seriously, give you assurance that you are not alone in this world, and challenge you to be all that God created you to be.

Daily prayer doesn't require you to step out of your life. If you forget or stop for whatever reason, you can simply start again, without a lot of guilt or concern that you're a bad person, because you're not. You don't have to be an expert at daily prayer. Given all its benefits, incredibly enough, daily prayer doesn't take a lot of time. In fact, it's good to start small. Prayer's fruitfulness comes not in the length of our prayers, but in our faithfulness to them.

Here is one way you might begin, or begin again: find a small bit of time each day to sit, or walk, or ride your bike, or drive in your car in silence. No ear buds. No radio or TV. No video games. No texting or social media. Start with ten minutes if you can. After a while, you'll want more than ten, but ten is a good place to start.

In those ten minutes, do two things. First, empty your mind by saying out loud all the things that you're thinking about, maybe worried about, and all that you want to have happen, wish were true, or are grateful for. Ask, specifically, for what you want or need. Ask for help. Ask for guidance. Jesus loved to tell stories to encourage us in prayer: about a woman who hounded a judge, or a man who banged on his friend's door late at night. Be persistent, Jesus said. "Ask, and it will be given to you; search, and you will find; knock, and the door will be opened for you" (Luke 11:5–10).

This is the first step in an honest, open relationship with God. It's important to be completely truthful. There is nothing to be gained in trying to be more religious than you are. Nor is there anything you can say or do that will be shocking to God. There is no inappropriate topic in prayer. You don't have to clean up your language or pretend to be someone you're not. In the gospels, Jesus is portrayed as one who loved talking with all manner of people, especially those regarded as sinners. Nor does it matter if you aren't sure on a given day that anyone is listening as you're talking. You needn't worry about the doubts that seem their strongest as you sit down to pray. We all have doubts sometimes. Nor is it unusual if you don't know how to imagine God—or to even wonder if God exists—as you're praying.

Jesus, not surprisingly, has helpful advice on how we might imagine God when we pray. The image he himself used most frequently when he prayed was that of a loving parent. He addressed God using the word *Abba*, which is an intimate, affectionate word for father in his language. Jesus wants us to think of God as a heavenly parent who always loves us, no matter what. Among his most well-known parables is that of a wayward son welcomed unconditionally home by a loving, forgiving father—the clear message being that we are all unconditionally loved (Luke 15:11–32).

I don't think this means that God is a man, as your biological father is a man. So if *father* is a troublesome metaphor for you, you can imagine God as a kind, generous and unconditionally loving mother. Jesus sometimes used feminine images of God. Male or female, the image is simply one of someone who truly loves you, and like the father in Jesus's story is always willing to meet you far more than halfway.

The second image Jesus offers to us as we pray is of himself, as the one who gave his life for us. He spoke of himself as the good shepherd who calls us each by name. He assures us that he is our way, our truth, and our light. As he shared his last meal with his disciples and was preparing them for his death, he said to them "You are my friends." Think of me, he says to us, as you would a really good friend, one who always has your back and your best interest at heart. After the Resurrection he told his disciples, "I am with you always, even to the end of the age." He is with us now.

Let's return to your time of prayer. First, put to words what is on your heart and mind. If you're feeling great about something, let God know, and offer thanks. If you've got a big decision to make and need guidance, ask for help. If you're feeling embarrassed or ashamed or foolish or worried, give voice to those feelings as well. If you're concerned for someone else, or saddened by whatever's happening in the world, bring those concerns to God.

When we speak to God in this way, we're not telling God anything that God doesn't already know. What's important in prayer is that we speak our truth and invite God into our lives. We know that prayer isn't magic. More often than not, the answer to our prayer isn't granting us what we want, but giving us the grace to accept what we cannot change. Paul famously describes an experience of prayer when he prayed for God to remove what he called a thorn in his side. "Three times I appealed to the Lord about this, that it would leave me, but he said to me, 'My grace is sufficient for you, for power is made perfect in weakness'" (2 Cor. 12:7–9). It is perhaps both the hardest and most affirming answer to prayer that God can give, telling us our task is to accept what we wish to be taken from us, and that we will be given sufficient strength to do so.

When I pray from my places of greatest need or vulnerability regarding the situations I cannot change and struggle to accept, what sometimes comes to me is the grace of God's compassion. In prayer, I don't have to pretend that whatever I'm up against is easy, and no longer do I feel shame for my struggle. In prayer, I receive a bit of strength to carry on, and sometimes the gift of new insight. Invariably, when I try to take matters into my own hands and try again to fix what is outside my control, I feel God's grace waiting for me to recover from yet another failed effort.

Patient Listening

After giving voice to all that is in my heart, I find it helpful to intentionally shift the conversation by saying aloud some version of what a wise old priest named Eli said to a young boy, Samuel, who kept hearing a voice call him in the night: "Speak Lord, for your servant is listening." Samuel's story, if you've not heard it before, is found in the biblical book that bears his name. He was a miracle baby, born to a previously barren woman, Hannah. In thanksgiving for the gift of her child, she entrusted him to Eli, a priest in the temple of the Lord. One night, Samuel heard his name called, and he ran to Eli thinking the priest had called him. But Eli sent him back to his bed, assuring him that he did not call. This happened two more times: the boy heard a voice and ran to Eli saying, "Here I am, for you called me." Then Eli realized that the Lord was calling the boy. He then told Samuel, "Go, lie down, and if he calls you, you shall say, speak Lord for your servant is listening" (I Sam. 3:1–9).

However we invite the Lord to speak to us, what remains for us in prayer is to wait. If your experience is anything like mine, waiting in silence requires patience. You may not hear anything at all. Rarely will you receive an immediate response, although it can happen. It almost never happens in my prayer, but I can remember vividly the few occasions I have heard God's response right away. Once when I was struggling to keep my head above water in all areas of my life, I cried out in prayer, "Is it always going to be this hard?" To my astonishment, the answer was immediate: "Yes." I burst out laughing. Then I heard, "But I will be with you."

Those words from God in prayer were enough to keep me going through one of the most challenging seasons of my life. When hard times return, I try to remember the time when God told me to expect hardship, but that God also promised to be with me. When I am feeling particularly weak, I try to remember what Paul wrote about God's power most fully revealed in human weakness (2 Cor. 12:9).

More often what I hear from God comes slowly, over time. *Hearing* may not be the right word for the experience. It's more like a sensation or a feeling, sometimes even a source of tension. I've learned that whatever it is I sense or feel, it's important to pay attention, and to act on whatever I have received. While I never know if what I'm perceiving is truly of God, I've learned that I have fewer regrets when I act on what comes to me in prayer than when I don't act.

The "speak Lord, for your servant is listening" part of the conversation with God can be challenging for another reason. When I allow myself to be quiet, other voices in my head can get very loud. Martin Laird likens our inner chaos to "a wild cocktail party of which we find ourselves the embarrassed host." The inner voices can be trivial, but they are often harsh and judgmental. Some are self-justifying; most are the fruit of anxiety. I can't always determine on my own, which, if any, of those voices are from God. I've learned that it's good to talk with someone with wisdom and experience in these matters—a trusted spiritual mentor or a good friend—to help in this discerning work.

I try to remember the words of Presiding Bishop Curry: "If the voice I hear, or the sensation I feel, is not one of love, then it is not of God." This isn't to suggest that God is a pushover or easily fooled by my self-deceptions, but that God's voice through Jesus's presence will always be one of love. It will call forth the best from us and gently correct us whenever we settle for a lesser version of ourselves.

I heard the chastising voice of God not long ago. When in conversation with a friend I said something about another person that was less than kind. In retrospect, I realized that I only said what I did to impress my friend and sound witty at another person's expense. When I thought back on that exchange in my time of prayer, the feeling that came over me was sadness. The question surfaced in my mind: "How would you feel if someone spoke in that way about you?" I rose from prayer resolved to be more careful with my speech.

Something else can happen in your quiet time of prayer: you may hear or sense a claim on your life, what in religious language is known as a call. It feels a bit like a summons. It's remarkably clear when the call comes, and it is often about something that needs to be done. It could be anything, large or small: call your mother, or sister, or next-door neighbor—now. Or, it could be a prodding to take the next step toward an unspoken dream or emerging potential, such as applying for a new job, completing a graduate school application you've been putting off, or inviting a person you admire for coffee. While it's easy to talk yourself out of following through on what you heard, in my experience there's nothing abstract or ambiguous about these bits of clarity when they surface in prayer. As you grow accustomed to the experience, you grow more confident in following where the summons may take you, allowing what you receive in prayer to be one of the guiding lights of your life.

The Practice of Prayer

Again, what I have learned, and continue to relearn, is that simply the practice of sitting quietly, speaking and listening to God with your heart, doesn't require a lot of time. As with most things of importance, what matters is consistency. In this way, the practice of prayer is like other daily practices necessary to sustain health in my life. I can skip those practices, one day or two, even for a week or month. Skip a year, and I put my health at risk. In prayer, what I risk losing without regular practice is a gentle awareness of God's daily presence and the gifts of calm, clarity, and direction that daily practice can provide. "The only way we can make time to pray," the former archbishop of Canterbury Rowan Williams gently reminds us, "is to make time to pray."[7]

---

7. Rowan Williams, private address to the Episcopal Diocese of Washington, St. Alban's Episcopal Church, November 8, 2018.

I also know that there can be long stretches of time when it feels impossible to find even ten minutes a day for intentional prayer. Or it may be that you have the time but can't bring yourself to sit still. Here's what I know: God understands. God does not judge, and will gladly meet you on the run. Some of my most powerful experiences in prayer have been in those times when I simply couldn't do my part, and Jesus showed up for me, wherever I was. That was especially true in the years I was parenting young children and working full time. There simply was no time, yet I often felt upheld by grace. Similarly, in the months after my father's death, I couldn't bring myself to sit and pray, and yet I never felt apart from God.

What I learned to do in those times was to pray intentionally while doing something else. I would pray as I was preparing a meal for my family, driving in the car, or working on a project. In particularly busy seasons now, I ask for God's support and guidance as I feel no choice but to go from one thing to the next. But when life settles a bit, I find a chair, sit down, and start again.

Prayer is not the only practice that informs a life with God, but it is foundational. It is also a practice, like the others in the Way of Love, which means that in prayer there is always room for growth. It's never too late to start or begin again. Daily, simple prayer will help you experience the fruits of faith, as you deepen your relationship with God through Jesus. In daily prayer, you learn to recognize Jesus's voice.

In the Way of Love, the practice of prayer fits alongside the first two practices: to turn and to learn. The three are easily practiced together. I try to begin each day by turning my attention to Jesus before I turn it toward anything else. I strive to set aside time before leaving the house or tending to the tasks of the day to sit in a chair that I've designated as my prayer chair. I set a timer for twenty minutes then settle into a time of learning and prayer. First, I generally read from the Bible. Then I say, or write, all that's on my heart, and I listen, as best I can.

This happens to be the rhythm of practice that suits my life now. It wasn't a rhythm I could sustain when I was raising children and working full time. In those years, I said most of my prayers on the run, as I was moving from one responsibility to the next. Your prayer rhythm will most certainly be different from mine, and it, too, will likely change as your life's rhythm changes. What's important is for each one of us to discover the rhythm or patterns that work for us in our lives as they are now. There's no formula that works for everyone. On the other hand, we don't need to start completely from scratch. Some spiritual practices are tested and true.

One of the greatest gifts in a life of prayer is reassurance that God sees us, as we are, and responds with love. We can be fully ourselves before God, not as we strive to be seen by others, but whom God alone knows us to be. As Richard Foster writes:

> The truth of the matter is we all come to prayer with a tangled mass of motives—altruistic and selfish, merciful and hateful, loving and bitter. Frankly, this side of eternity we will never unravel the good from the bad, the pure from the impure. But what I have come to see is that God is big enough to receive us with all our mixture. We do not have to be bright, or pure, or filled with faith, or anything.[8]

Such acceptance from God, especially in those times when I know I am in need of grace, enables me, albeit imperfectly, to offer a bit of grace to others. That acceptance may be among the greatest gifts of all: the fruits of a life transformed by God's love.

---

8. Foster, 8.

4

To Worship

> For I received from the Lord what I also handed on to you, that the Lord Jesus on the night when he was betrayed took a loaf of bread, and when he had given thanks, he broke it and said, "This is my body that is for you. Do this in remembrance of me." In the same way he took the cup also, after supper, saying, "This cup is the new covenant in my blood. Do this, as often as you drink it, in remembrance of me." For as often as you eat this bread and drink the cup, you proclaim the Lord's death until he comes. —1 Corinthians 11:23–26

THE SEVEN PRACTICES in the Way of Love find their origin in ancient disciplines that the earliest followers of Jesus adopted and passed down to future generations. The Way of Love thus invites us to experience in new ways the practices that have sustained Christians for centuries. This is especially true as we move now to the fourth practice, to *worship*. The impulse to worship is intrinsic to our human nature and has been from the origin of our species.

World religion scholar Karen Armstrong writes in her comprehensive history of religion, *A History of God*:

Men and women started to worship gods as soon as they became recognizably human: they created religions at the same time as they created works of art. This is not simply because they wanted to propitiate powerful forces: these early faiths expressed the wonder and mystery that seem always to have been an essential component of the human experience of this beautiful yet terrifying world.[1]

The form and structure of Christian worship finds its roots in Jewish synagogue and temple rituals and the table fellowship of Jesus's earliest followers. Jesus's last Passover meal with his disciples is the symbolic touchstone for Christians, a ritual in which we not only remember but symbolically reenact that meal. Doing so we place ourselves around the table Jesus sets for us and share in the mystery of his presence among us when we gather.

The Way of Love unapologetically affirms the spiritual importance of gathering weekly with other Christians around Jesus's table. The spiritual practice of worship is, by definition, communal. While worship via technology has become a widespread and spiritually meaningful experience for many, the Way of Love encourages us to show up physically to worship weekly with other people in a house of prayer. Of course, there are times in life when showing up for communal worship is impossible, and worship via technology allows us to stay connected to other Christians during those times. However, the gift of worshipping with others in the flesh and the opportunities for spiritual growth it affords are pearls of great price, well worth the effort and sacrifice required to fully experience them. My focus here is on what lies at the center of a particular type of Christian worship found in sacramental faith traditions, including the Episcopal Church.

---

1. Karen Armstrong, *A History of God: The 4,000-Year Quest of Judaism, Christianity, and Islam* (New York: Random House, 1993), xix.

The word *sacrament* refers to rituals that are both symbols and portals of experience for a particular grace that only God can give. The Christian sacrament at the heart of worship is known in most Episcopal churches as *Eucharist*, a Greek word for thanksgiving, which refers to our reenactment of Jesus's last meal with his disciples. In other sacramental churches this sacred meal is referred to as Holy Communion, the Lord's Supper, or the Mass. Eucharist symbolizes and invites us to participate in Jesus's sacrificial love for all humankind. Moreover, there is at the heart of Eucharist the conviction that Jesus is present with us as he promised he would be: "Remember, I am with you always, to the end of the age" (Matt. 28:20).

In Eucharist, we recite the ancient story of the fateful night before his death. We hear for ourselves the words Jesus spoke: "Take, eat; this is my body, which is given for you. Do this in remembrance of me." "This cup that is poured out for you is the new covenant in my blood" (Luke 22:19–20).

The mystical power of Eucharist explains why it became the central focus of worship whenever Jesus's followers gathered. The earliest records of Christian practice include this reenacted meal, because in it our spiritual forebears felt his presence with them. Over two thousand years later, so can we.

On the Road to Emmaus

The most poignant biblical account of the first disciples' experience of his presence while sharing bread and wine isn't that of the last supper itself, but rather an account of what happened to two of the disciples shortly after Jesus's crucifixion. We find that story in the Gospel of Luke. It tells of what happened on the day of Jesus's resurrection, which these two individuals could not yet grasp in their grief of his crucifixion.

As the story begins, two of the twelve have left Jerusalem and set out on the road to a town called Emmaus. Earlier that morning, the women among Jesus's disciples had gone to his tomb and breathlessly returned with stories of angels, the tomb being empty, and more amazingly still, that Jesus was alive. Two of the men—we aren't told which ones—couldn't make sense of what the women told them. They did what many of us do, to paraphrase Yeats, "when there's a fire in our heads."[2] They went for a walk. The destination was unimportant; they simply needed to get out of town.

While they were on the road Jesus appeared to them, but they didn't recognize him. He walked at their side, listened to their grief, and slowly began to reveal himself to them, as he often does to us, through the stories of scripture. They still didn't know who he was, but later, they realized that as he spoke their hearts were "strangely warmed." When evening came, they begged him to stay with them at a roadside lodge. While they were at table with him, he took the bread and blessed it, as he'd done that final night of his life. Then the disciples recognized him at last, and he disappeared from their sight (Luke 24:13–35).

It's been said that for those who follow Jesus, every road is a road to Emmaus. This is because we're all on the road to somewhere, and he's with us, but most of the time we don't recognize him. He is hidden in the people we meet, in the events of our lives and of the world, and even within ourselves in ways that we don't always feel. But once a week, Christians make the effort to show up in church. In community with others, we focus our attention on Jesus. We hear stories read aloud from his life and his teachings. Someone takes the time, as Jesus did for the disciples on the road, to interpret the texts to us, bringing them into conversation with our lives. Sometimes when a person is speaking, we hear Jesus's

---

2. William Butler Yeats, "The Song of Wandering Aengus" in *The Wind Among the Reeds* (1899), *https://www.poetryfoundation.org/poems/55687/the-song-of-wandering-aengus* (accessed February 19, 2019).

voice speaking. We feel his presence. How does that happen? I don't know. It is the mystery of faith.

As the worship experience continues, we gather around a table symbolizing the table of his last supper. We relive the story of that fateful meal, and then take part in it, symbolically, sacramentally. As we do, we feel his presence, not all the time, not every Sunday, but often enough to trust it. To the outsider, the meal is no more than a sacred symbol. But to the believer, the very definition of a sacrament means entering into the living, breathing, and blessing life of God in our own time and in our own terms.

We're told that once the disciples on the road to Emmaus recognized Jesus, he disappeared from their sight. I believe it, because my own moments of connection and experiences of his presence are also fleeting. Nor are these experiences something I can evoke on command—none of us can. But when we experience his presence, when Jesus is real for us, in words spoken, prayers offered, and bread and wine shared among a community gathered, it's enough to give us hope, courage, and the assurance that we're loved.

The Gift of Christian Community

Jesus wants us to invite others to the table, so that they, too, might experience his presence with them and love for them. Sometimes we in the church mistakenly assume that what we have to offer others in worship is ourselves. "We're a great church," we tell ourselves, and no doubt we are. Our presence is important, as is the authenticity of our welcome and vibrancy of our spiritual life. But what sets Christian community apart from any other gathering is Jesus's presence at the heart of our worship. He is, to paraphrase a beloved hymn, "our Way, our Truth, our Life."[3] Because we share

---

3. "Come, My Way, My Truth, My Life," *The Hymnal, 1982* (New York: Church Hymnal, 1982), hymn 487.

the experience of his presence, we feel a particular bond with one another. That is the gift of Christian community.

In 2004 Marcus Borg published a book entitled *The Heart of Christianity: Rediscovering a Life of Faith.* I was serving as a parish priest at the time, and his book so impressed me that I gave it to everyone I knew who wanted to know what it meant be a follower of Jesus. It remains a book that I return to for insight and inspiration.

In a chapter on spiritual practice entitled "The Heart of the Matter," Borg wrote something about communal worship that I've never forgotten. By way of background, for Marcus Borg, Christianity is most fruitfully experienced and understood as a way of life rather than a system of belief. Beliefs are important, but when we assume that Christianity is primarily about accepting as true a belief system, we risk placing too much emphasis on what we think or feel rather than how we live. It is through living the Christian life that we are given insights and experiences that take root within us as a core conviction.

Anne Lamott says much the same thing in an essay entitled "Why I Make Sam Go to Church." Her son was nine years old at the time of her writing, and her reason for making him to go church was simply this:

> I want to give him what I found in the world, which is to say a path and a little light to see by. Most of the people I know who have what I want—which is to say, purpose, heart, balance, gratitude, joy—are people with a deep sense of spirituality. They are people in community, who pray, or practice their faith; they are Buddhists, Jews, Christians—people banding together to work on themselves and for human rights. They follow a brighter light than the glimmer of their own candle; they are part of something beautiful. . . . Our funky little church is filled with people who are working for peace and freedom, who are out there on the

streets and inside praying, and they are home writing letters, and they are at the shelters with giant platters of food. [4]

For Borg and Lamott, the earliest title for Christians rings true: we are "People of the Way" (Acts 9:2). This Way, Borg writes in *The Heart of Christianity*, is comprised of practices that help us to pay attention to God and be open to receive the presence of Jesus. Practices form our identity and shape our character. They hold us accountable, just as practices in other areas of our life do, and, importantly, practices nourish us. They feed our souls.

In his chapter on spiritual practice, Borg emphatically states that the single most important spiritual practice is to be part of a congregation that, in his words, "nourishes you even as it stretches you." He offers this bit of advice:

> Some of you are already involved in such a church. But if you are not involved in any church or are part of one that leaves you hungry and unsatisfied, find one that nourishes and deepens your Christian journey. Find one that makes your heart glad, so that you wake up on Sunday morning with the anticipation of the psalmist, "I was glad when they said to me, 'Let us go to the house of the Lord.'" Choosing a church is not primarily about feeling good, but church is meant to nourish us, not to make us angry or leave us bored. If your church gives you a headache, it may be time to change.[5]

I first read that passage as the pastor and priest of a small congregation, with all the joys and struggles of church life. As I read, I felt a light go off in my head. For I knew that I wanted, more than anything, to help nurture and sustain a church that

---

4. Anne Lamott, *Traveling Mercies: Some Thoughts on Faith* (New York: Random House, 2000), 101.

5. Marcus Borg, *The Heart of Christianity: Rediscovering the Heart of Faith* (New York: HarperOne, 2004), 194.

made people's hearts glad. I wanted the people in the congregation I served to wake up on Sunday morning looking forward to church. I didn't want to lead a church that was boring or, God forbid, gave people headaches. I wanted to lead a church that nourishes people and deepens their Christian journey. I still do, and I believe that when church leaders keep that focus, Christian community thrives.

I'm not suggesting that we're always glad, or that church doesn't have its challenges. Churches are filled with human beings, all of us broken in our own ways, all dealing with real challenges in our lives and in the world around us. The gift of a church community, and at its core the gift of worship, is that we can bring all of ourselves and our lives—the full catastrophe—to Jesus's table, and rise from our worship blessed.

If you're not part of a worshipping community, I urge to you to take Borg's words to heart. Find one, large or small, regardless of faith tradition, that makes your heart glad. I want you to wake up on Sunday, happy that it is a day for you to attend church. If you're among those feeling exhausted, stressed, or empty in your church experience, pay attention to what God might be saying to you. While I would hope, for the church's sake, that you feel called to stay and make things better, if that's too much of a burden, look for a church that feeds your soul.

Finding a church that feels like home is a bit like falling in love. You can approach the endeavor with a checklist of all the things you're looking for and feel you need in a church, as you might a potential mate. Your list could express both needs and longings, but the Holy Spirit might surprise you. You might feel called to a church with very few, if any, of the qualities on your list. That happened to me a few times in my life when I was free to search for a spiritual community: the Holy Spirit led me to a church I would never have chosen on my own. I had made a list of all the qualities I was looking for in a church, but the church I eventually joined didn't have any of them. Nonetheless, as soon as I walked in, I felt drawn to the community in ways that defied logic. When walking on the road to Emmaus, we never know where the journey will lead.

For those of us who are leaders of a church community, Borg's words are an invitation for honest assessment. How does our worship nurture the souls of those present? As bishop, I worship in a different congregation every Sunday. Every week, I try to assess what I've come to call "the joy quotient" in worship. I look around and ask myself, "How uplifting is the worship experience? Are people singing? Are they smiling as they sing? Do those who read the biblical texts do so in compelling ways? How does it feel when we gather around Jesus's table?" Particularly with words that we repeat each week, it matters that we wholeheartedly engage them, giving life to the words that Jesus entrusts to us.

One final question, specifically now for church leaders: how would you describe your worship environment in terms of cleanliness, sense of welcome, and comfort? To be frank, I'm often dismayed by the amount of clutter I see in our worship spaces and throughout our church buildings, and how little effort is made to ensure our worship is inviting to those unfamiliar with our traditions. There are so many small things we can do to create a warm and welcoming space in which people can relax and thus open themselves to experience the loving presence of Jesus. Tending to them as leaders is our way of creating sacred space and offering our best selves, so that Jesus may have more to work with and through when we gather.

Claiming the Time

I close this chapter with a word of encouragement to all who are part of a worshipping community, or long to be, but feel the constant pull of other commitments that conspire to take you away from a weekly practice of worship. I understand. We live in a 24/7 world, and Sunday is no longer a day of rest in our culture, if it ever was. I understand the pressures of work and relationships, and the competing claims on small windows of discretionary time.

In response, all I can say is that regular worship with other Christians in a spiritually nourishing environment is food for your soul and a priceless opportunity to experience the presence of Christ in community. Worship is important but rarely urgent. Other claims on our time will almost always feel as if they need to take precedence, and perhaps at times they do. But what is lost when a weekly rhythm of worship is missing is hard to regain. You may not notice it at first, but over time the absence of communal spiritual sustenance will take its toll. It's not that we can't experience Jesus's love elsewhere, but there is a particular grace in worship—an abiding presence known to us over time—that is worth the effort to be present each week.

What's more, there are times when we need to be in worship for someone else's sake. In worship, as in other places, we're sometimes given the chance to be a living expression of God's love for another, as others are for us. It's a powerful experience when we're aware of what's happening, yet we're often unaware of how we help others feel Jesus's presence with and for them. Should they later tell us of our part in their sacred encounters, we may not even remember what it was that we said or did. Surely the fact that we can be expressions of God's love for one another adds another motivation to be present in worship even when it would be easier to stay home. Not only do we experience God's grace in worship for ourselves, we could very well play a part in the answer to someone else's prayer.

May God bless each of us as we walk our road to Emmaus, where Jesus meets us, often without our recognizing him. May we all experience those brief, powerful encounters as we gather in worship and he reveals himself to us, in scripture and the breaking of the bread.

5

{~~·~~}

To Bless

SHARE FAITH AND UNSELFISHLY GIVE AND SERVE

> Then the righteous will answer him, "Lord, when was it that we saw you hungry and gave you food, or thirsty and gave you something to drink? And when was it that we saw you a stranger and welcomed you, or naked and gave you clothing? And when was it that we saw you sick or in prison and visited you?" And the king will answer them, "Truly I tell you, just as you did it to one of the least of these who are members of my family, you did it to me." —Matthew 25:37–40

TO BLESS IS THE MOST AFFIRMING and life-giving of all the practices, as much for us as when we offer blessing to others. In acts and expressions of blessing, we share in the creative love of God that has blessed us all from the beginning of creation. God is the primary source of all blessing, all that is good and lovely and life-affirming in this world. Our lives are immeasurably enriched with daily opportunities to offer and receive blessings. Simply holding the words *bless* and *blessing* in our awareness opens us to opportunities to offer and receive blessing that we might otherwise miss. The joy of blessing is contagious.

The words *bless* and *blessing* show up with some regularity in ordinary speech. For example, whenever anyone sneezes in our presence, we automatically respond by saying, "God bless you." Have you ever wondered why? Virtually every culture in the world has some phrase of blessing in response to a sneeze. Pope Gregory the Great of the sixth century is given credit as the first person to say "God bless you" when someone sneezed. It was no small blessing, for a severe plague had spread across Europe and sneezing was one of its symptoms. While we now know that sneezing doesn't necessarily mean that we're sick, the impulse remains to wish sneezers good health.

Another common usage of the words *bless* and *blessing* is what we say, often in prayer, before eating a meal. This, too, is a universal practice. Christian blessings usually direct our focus to the food itself, to those who prepared it, and to those who will partake. You may know this prayer: "Bless these gifts to our use and us to thy loving service, Amen." In Jewish table prayers, which would have been Jesus's tradition, the words of blessing are directed to God: "Blessed are You, Lord our God, Ruler of the universe, for you bring forth bread from the earth. Blessed are You, Lord our God, Ruler of the universe, for you create the fruit of the vine."

However we say our blessing and whatever our focus, to bless encourages mindfulness and gratitude for the gift of food. It helps us remember that no matter how self-reliant we are, we are also dependent on the source of all life for our life. To receive from that source is a gift, one that inspires us to give more generously in return.

A third way that words of blessing are used in common speech is in response to a question used as a form of greeting: "How are you?" Among the typical answers we give are, "I'm fine, how are you?" or "Not bad, thanks," or this more uplifting reply, "I'm blessed."

What does it mean when we respond to a standard question of greeting by saying that we're blessed? That life is going well, perhaps, or that we feel surrounded by good fortune. What's striking to me about the response, "I'm blessed," is that it doesn't seem to depend on the outer circumstances of life. People will say they are feeling blessed not only in good times, but also in the hardest of circumstances. In the midst of a devastating illness, people will say they are blessed by the love of their family or the care of their doctors. Others who have lost a loved one will give thanks for the blessing of their church community or the friends that are carrying them through.

The Practice of Blessing

Much of the kindness we naturally offer one another is blessing by another name. To recognize such gestures as a spiritual practice simply encourages us to become more adept at blessing, being mindful that we are instruments of God's love when we do. I'd like to describe three ways that the practice of blessing can draw us closer to God and help us grow in our capacity to love.

The first is perhaps the most obvious: we bless others whenever we choose to offer concrete expressions of kindness to someone who is in need or pain. In such instances it matters that we act and not merely speak our blessing. As the Apostle James makes clear: "If a brother or sister is naked and lacks daily food, and one of you says to them, 'Go in peace; keep warm and eat your fill,' and yet you do not supply their bodily needs, what is the good of that?" (James 2:15–16).

Jesus makes the same point in a parable he told about the final judgment of humankind, when God will separate people from one another as a shepherd separates sheep from goats. Those who will receive the ultimate blessing of God are those who blessed others with deeds of compassion. Unbeknownst to them at the time, they were also blessing God. "Truly I tell you, just as you did it to one of the least of these who are members of my family, you did it to me" (Matt. 25:40). One of the hallmarks of this form of blessing is kindness. As John O'Donohue writes, "When someone is kind to you, you feel understood and seen.

There is no judgement or harsh perception directed towards you. Kindness has gracious eyes."[1]

Not long ago I had a bicycle accident. While riding on a trail alongside Rock Creek Parkway in Washington, D.C., my handlebars caught a bush on the left side of the trail, causing my wheels to slip from under me. I fell hard on the pavement, my head just inches from the road and oncoming cars. I lay on the trail as people rode their bikes and drove their cars by without stopping. All I could think of was the story Jesus told about a wounded man on the roadside (Luke 10:25–37). I wondered if anyone would stop.

As in Jesus's story, eventually someone did stop and asked if I was injured. She stayed long enough to make sure that I was all right, which apart from a few scratches and a sore right side, I was. Only when I convinced her that I truly was fine did she continue on her way.

I felt the blessing of her presence and sincere willingness to help. She didn't tell me her name, but I will never forget her kindness.

The next day I attended a dedication service for a tuition-free school for boys sponsored by the Diocese of Washington named in honor of the late Bishop John Walker. The school's mission is to provide a high-quality education to African American boys in the most underserved areas of Washington, D.C. The Bishop Walker School recently moved into a beautiful new facility housed within a large complex of arts, educational, and social service organizations in southeast Washington. We had gathered to celebrate this new chapter in the school's mission.

The ceremony began with one of the students standing to recite the Bishop Walker School prayer: "Grant, O Lord, in all the joys of this life we may never forget to be kind. Help us to be unselfish in

---

1. John O'Donohue, *To Bless the Space Between Us: A Book of Blessings* (New York: Doubleday, 2008), 186.

friendship, thoughtful to those less happy than ourselves, and eager to bear the burdens of others." Thirty students then sang a musical rendition of that prayer. As I looked into the teary, smiling faces of those gathered for the dedication, most of whom had been financial supporters since the school's inception, I realized that endeavors like the Bishop Walker School are only possible when individual people decide to strategically and collectively invest in blessing. For blessings to last generations, they must be embedded in institutions whose mission is to bless. We can't possibly accomplish sustained large-scale blessing on our own, but we can whenever we collectively invest our energies and resources.

A second way we can practice blessing is related to the Christian ritual known as *benediction*. A benediction is an official blessing, spoken on God's behalf, typically by an ordained minister at the end of a church service or other ceremony. Benedictions are common throughout the Bible, generally as the last words spoken by a revered leader, or at the beginning or the end of a text. In each of these contexts, the words are meant to give reassurance and encouragement, or to convey a sense of joy, peace, and affirmation.

Here are two familiar examples from the Bible: "The Lord bless you and keep you; the Lord make his face to shine upon you and be gracious to you; the Lord lift up his countenance upon you and give you peace." This was an ancient Jewish blessing, originally spoken by Aaron, Moses's brother, as recorded in the book of Numbers (6:22–26). Another beloved Christian blessing is found at the beginning of Paul's letter to the Christians in Philippi: "I thank my God every time I remember you, constantly praying with joy in every one of my prayers for all of you, because of your sharing in the gospel from the first day until now. I am confident of this, that the one who began a good work among you will bring it to completion by the day of Jesus Christ" (Phil. 1:3–6).

As beautiful as official benedictions can be, the authority to bless is not reserved only for religious leaders to be said in ceremonial contexts. We can all do this, anywhere, anytime. John O'Donohue dedicated his life to retrieving the lost art form and practice of blessing, which he defined as "words that create a circle of light drawn around a person to protect, and strengthen."[2] For him, the word itself evokes a sense of warmth and protection. "It suggests that no life is alone and unreachable."[3] We can create circles of light around one another with words of kindness and affirmation.

Here's what the spiritual practice of blessing looks like for me. When I'm in conversation with others—be they family members, coworkers, neighbors, or friends—at the point of saying goodbye, I try to offer a word of affirmation and encouragement. I'll point out, for example, some quality that I see in them that I love or admire. Or I'll reflect back to something they had said in the conversation as a statement of courage or love. If they're going through a hard time, I acknowledge that fact and try to let them know that I'm here for them. I tell them how much they mean to me. I try not to overdo this, for the goal here is not to shower people with false praise but go deep within and speak from the heart.

Blessing is a wonderfully uplifting practice and a reminder of the importance of our words. As Joan Chittister writes: "The godly are those who never talk destructively about another person—in anger, in spite, in vengefulness. They can be counted on to bring an open heart to a closed and clawing world. . . . The holy ones are those who live well with those around them. They are just, they are upright, they are kind. The ecology of humankind is safe with them."[4]

As I've deepened this practice of late, I've discovered that I am also more open to receive words of affirmation that others speak to me, rather than dismiss their words in embarrassment or false

---

2. O'Donohue, *To Bless the Space*, 198.

3. O'Donohue, ibid., xiii.

4. Chittister, 24.

humility. For example, my eighty-seven-year-old mother concludes almost every conversation with, "I'm so proud of you." It's always made me feel awkward. But now I say to myself, "Take it in, Mariann. Feel the blessing." I encourage you to do the same.

Blessings during Hardship

The third practice of blessing is the most difficult, given its context. I touched upon it earlier when reflecting on what we mean when we say "I'm blessed," no matter our circumstance. Part of this spiritual practice is learning how to accept the blessing that comes to us in situations we would have given anything to avoid. I have never believed that God brings hardship and suffering upon us, but I know from experience and observation of others that we can, nonetheless, feel blessed in difficult times. To name those blessings for ourselves has the power to transform our experience of suffering.

Blessings born of hardship are all around us, such as when in the midst of natural disaster, a community pulls together and people care for one another in transformative ways, forever changing the quality of life going forward for the better. Blessings during difficult times also take the form of deep, inner transformation. We need never feel grateful for the heartbreaking events that provided soil for the blessing to take root in order to give thanks for its flowering in our lives. As noted Episcopal priest and author Barbara Brown Taylor writes,

> It was when your family moved for the fourth time in five years that you learned to enjoy your own company in the months before you made new friends. It was when your partner left you that you remembered what else you meant to do in your life beyond staying together. It was when the doctor called you about the spot on your lung that you finally made up with your sister. These were not the ways you would have chosen to become

more than you were, but they worked. Pain burned up the cushions you used to keep from hitting bottom.[5]

To be sure not all hardships bring about blessing in this way. Some are too devastating. Moreover, our response to pain matters, how willing and able we are to seek out and claim blessing wrought by pain.

There's a famous story in Genesis of a long and lonely night when a man named Jacob wrestled with a stranger, whom he later referred to as an angel. Jacob was, by all accounts, a scoundrel. Early in his life he stole the blessing his father intended to give to his brother Esau. In ancient Israel a father's blessing, once spoken, could not be retrieved, even in the case of mistaken identity, as it was with Jacob and Esau. You can imagine how well the two brothers got along after that.

The stolen blessing, while real, did not sit well with Jacob's conscience. He knew that he needed to reconcile with his brother, which he eventually did. He also knew that somehow, he had to come clean with God. It was during that time of internal struggle, when Jacob had fled with his family and camped out near a stream, that the strange man appeared and wrestled with him all night long. It was a physical expression of Jacob's inner torment. Finally, at daybreak, when the man asked Jacob to let him go, Jacob replied, "I will not let you go unless you bless me" (Gen. 32:22–31).

"I will not let you go unless you bless me," is one of my favorite lines in all the Bible. We all must wrestle in life with hardships and struggles, our own failures and mistakes. We must wrestle with them until the blessing reveals itself. I am not suggesting that we sugarcoat something terrible, or pretend to feel blessed when we don't, but rather that we allow ourselves to receive blessing in our times of trial—however it comes. It could be the blessing of

---

5. Barbara Brown Taylor, *An Altar in the World: A Geography of Faith* (New York: HarperOne, 2009), 157.

a hard-won truth, or a capacity that's grown in us because of our experience, or a gift that sustains us through our ordeal. We would never wish what we have gone through on anyone, and yet the blessing, when it comes, is often enough for us to be grateful for the person we've become as a result of our trials. That is the miraculous power of blessing.

One way to appreciate the power of blessing is to imagine a day or a life without it. It's heartbreaking to contemplate being deprived or depriving oneself of the creative, transformative power to bless and receive blessing. Every year at Christmastime, Americans flock to theaters to see adaptations of *A Christmas Carol* by Charles Dickens. In that classic tale, Ebenezer Scrooge was a man who could neither give nor receive blessing. Though he had riches to spare, he was one to be pitied, even by those who suffered want or who endured his mindless cruelty. With the nighttime visitation of three ghosts who awakened his conscience and softened his heart, Scrooge was given a chance to redeem his life. The story ends joyously as Scrooge lavishly extends blessing and is embraced in the warmth of the family and friends he once shunned. Through blessing, Scrooge is born again.

To practice blessing is to keep our eyes and ears open for the opportunities to offer blessing, through our actions and our words, to one another and to receive in gratitude blessings offered us. In times of hardship or struggle, the practice of blessing is more like a prayer, asking God to reveal or provide the blessing we need or that a loved one might receive. I pray that when others ask, by way of greeting, "How are you?" you can say, in all sincerity, no matter the circumstance, "I'm blessed." What's more, I pray you know yourself to be a blessing, as one who creates circles of light and love for others through your words of affirmation and concrete expressions of Jesus's love. Such is the way of blessing. Such is the Way of Love.

6

✦

To Go

CROSS BOUNDARIES, LISTEN DEEPLY, AND LIVE LIKE JESUS

> "Which of these three, do you think, was a neighbor to the man who fell into the hands of the robbers?" He said, "The one who showed him mercy." Jesus said to him, "Go and do likewise." —Luke 10:36–37

IN EARLY DECEMBER 2019, I received an e-mail from a colleague. "I know this is a last-minute invitation," he wrote, "but a group of us are going to El Paso, Texas, next week to meet with our counterparts on both sides of the U.S./Mexico border, and if possible, with those seeking asylum in our country. Would you like to go with us?" My heart leapt and sank at the same time, and I thought, "If only my life would allow me to accept. But of course I can't." I immediately began to rationalize my decision to decline. "What good could possibly come from a few days' visit? I have deadlines to meet. There are countless concerns for me to address in my own city."

My immediate decision to say no did not sit well. In my heart, I wanted to go. Why was my head saying no? I looked at my calendar again and realized that it wouldn't be that difficult to move a few appointments. I began to wonder if this might be a holy invitation, perhaps even an imperative. I decided to test the

63

waters by speaking to those close to me. Those I had assumed would discourage me from going were grateful that I would even consider such a journey. "Please go," they said. "We want to hear about what you see."

Within a few hours, I had conferred with my husband, cleared my calendar, and booked a ticket to El Paso. A few days later, I found myself walking the same streets of Juarez, Mexico, that I had visited in high school, this time seeing the border through the eyes of those fleeing violence and extreme poverty in their homelands. We met with Christian organizations dedicated to providing shelter and legal support for migrants in El Paso. Our group prayed outside the juvenile detention center in Trujillo, Texas, where over three thousand unaccompanied minors are being held in a facility built for three hundred. I was alternately heartbroken and inspired at every turn: heartbroken at the human suffering and inspired by those dedicating their lives to alleviate it.

As we reflected on our experience and prayed together, members of our group considered ways we might return to El Paso in the future with material support and volunteers to help those who were doing all they could to assist the traumatized migrants. We wondered what we could say with our collective voice on the need for greater compassion in our nation's immigration policies. I returned home reminded of the power of proximity, how important it is to experience firsthand the sufferings and injustice I can all too easily keep at a safe distance, debating "the issues" of our time without personally knowing or engaging anyone adversely affected by them.

There is risk in going, a vulnerability in crossing boundaries that conspire to keep us separate from one another. Yet such risk is an expression of love. Our going activates love within and among us that would otherwise lie dormant. Paul writes in his letter to the Philippians (2:5–8) of Jesus's love as the ultimate border crossing and urges us to follow his example:

Let the same mind be in you that was in Christ Jesus, who, though he was in the form of God, did not regard equality with God as something to be exploited, but emptied himself, taking the form of a slave, being born in human likeness. And being found in human form, he humbled himself and became obedient to the point of death—even death on a cross.

Jesus is an expression of how far God is willing to go for our sake. Where are we willing to go in response to such love?

Yet we know that it isn't possible for us to go everywhere, all the time. In the face of sometimes overwhelming need, the question of discernment is always before us. How on earth are we to determine where God is calling us to go in the midst of seemingly endless possibilities? Sometimes out of guilt or a fear of missing something I assume that I should go to all manner of places, all of them worthwhile, all in response to a need or with important work to be done. Sometimes I go, far less certain of God's call than I am of my own need to be included or seen.

Thomas Merton, a monk and one of the wisest Christian writers of the twentieth century, dedicated his life to listening to God and helping others do the same. He once wrote a prayer confessing how little he knew about God's will for his life, and the particularly dangerous terrain he was in whenever he imagined that he did know:

O Lord God, I have no idea where I am going. I do not see the road ahead of me, I cannot know for certain where it will end. Nor do I really know myself, and the fact that I think I am following your will does not mean that I am actually doing so.[1]

Like Merton, we are wise to acknowledge our uncertainty about God's call to go, as we take one step and then another, making course corrections along the way.

---

1. Thomas Merton, *Thoughts in Solitude* (New York: Farrar, Straus, and Giroux, 1958), 83.

Sometimes I think we know exactly where God wants us to go, but we pretend that we don't. We pretend, we ignore, we do almost anything to avoid where we're being asked to go because, for a variety of reasons, we simply don't want to go there. I am acutely aware of reluctance to go to places where I feel out of control or where I fear being harshly judged. I also know that as one accustomed to the comforts of privilege, it's frightening to risk losing them. On a more mundane level, sometimes I say no out of laziness.

Saying "No" to Go

I wouldn't go so far as to say that "No" is always our response to God's call for us to go somewhere specific, but it's often our first response. There's a great story in the Bible—pure fiction, but true nonetheless—about a man who in response to the first time God asked him to go somewhere ran as far as he could in the opposite direction. His name was Jonah, and in the book that bears his name, we hear God tell Jonah to go to the city of Nineveh. His task is to preach a word of judgment, for the citizens of Nineveh have sinned greatly, and God is not pleased. Jonah doesn't want to go to Nineveh, because he doesn't like the people there, and it pleases him to think of them being punished for their misdeeds.

To avoid God's call Jonah runs away, eventually stowing himself on a boat that's going off to sea. A storm arises that causes the boat's crew to panic, and they throw Jonah overboard. You may recall that Jonah then finds himself in the belly of a large fish, where he remains for three days. That's long enough for him to realize that going wherever God asks him to go, however unpleasant, is better than remaining where he is. So he cries out to God, God hears him, and at God's command, the fish spits Jonah out.

Then, the text tells, "the Lord comes to Jonah a second time." When God tells Jonah to go to Nineveh this time, Jonah says yes. He goes and warns the people of Nineveh that they face God's judgment if they do not change their sinful ways. As Jonah feared, the people of Nineveh actually listen to him and begin the painful process of amending their lives. God, in turn, has mercy on them which irritates Jonah to no end, but despite his initial reluctance and bad attitude, Jonah went where God told him go. As a result, the people were spared.

The moral of the story of Jonah is that when God tells us to go somewhere, yes is a better answer than no, but getting to yes isn't always easy.

Saying no to God doesn't mean that we're bad people. It's understandable to resist a call to go places that seem risky or dangerous, or, less nobly on our part, merely inconvenient. We want to maintain control of our lives or the illusion of control. Sometimes, however, we say no not because we don't want to go, but because what God is asking is too much for us. If we could, we would go, but can't—at least not yet and not on our own strength. There's a story in one of the gospels of a rich young man who approached Jesus, asking him for guidance. Jesus immediately took a liking to him and invited him to sell all that he had and join Jesus's band of disciples. The young man couldn't do it, and heartbroken, he walked away. It broke Jesus's heart to see him go. "How hard it will be," he said, "for those who have wealth to enter the Kingdom of God" (Mark 10:17–27). I like to imagine that young man coming back to Jesus someday, or later joining the band of apostles.

I have the sense that God isn't surprised when at first, or for a long time, we say no when God asks us to go somewhere. God knows that what is being asked of us is hard and may well be beyond our capacity. Of course we say no at first. Think of Jesus in the Garden of Gethsemane. He knew where the path of faithfulness was taking him, but he didn't want to go there. "Father, if it is possible, let this cup pass from me," he prayed (Matt. 26:39). Sometimes we want the cup to pass from us, too.

Jesus went on to pray perhaps the hardest, most courageous, and yes, most submissive prayer of all: "But not my will; your will be done." Jesus submitted his will to God's will. I do my best to pray that prayer, but sometimes I can't. I may say the words but my heart isn't ready to accept what I would do anything to avoid. What I learned is that I am not condemned by my reluctance; Jesus invites me to stay in relationship, stay in conversation, to bring my concerns, fear, and even protests to God in prayer. Remember Jonah, arguably the most reluctant prophet in the Bible. Even in the belly of the fish, he stayed in conversation with God. "No" wasn't his final answer. It needn't be ours, either.

How, then, does God help us move from no to yes?

Saying "Yes" to Go

Looking back on my life, there have been times when God planted a seed of possibility for my future by asking me to go somewhere well before I could possibly say yes. Even in the times when I tried to go, I failed at first. Often God draws us in love to greater spiritual growth by inviting us to stretch farther than our spiritual maturity can do gracefully. As a result I learned important lessons from failure that prepared me for the next time I heard the call to go somewhere that was foreign or fearful to me. I also have watched friends and family members wrestle with an emerging sense of call—going back and forth, categorically saying no, or trying and failing, only to experience the same call surface again. The English poet Francis Thompson described this process as being pursued by "the hound of heaven."[2] It can feel as if we're being hounded, until finally we're ready to say, "Yes, I will go."

Another way that God coaxes us in love from no to yes is through the example of other people, and in particular, the people

---

2. Francis Thompson, *The Hound of Heaven*, https://www.bartleby.com/236/239.html (accessed February 20, 2019).

who inspire us. They encourage us precisely because they have crossed the threshold that could be our destiny. We see in them some unrealized potential in us, and we want to be where they are. We want to be like them, and part of us may even long to be them, which, of course, we can't. We can only be ourselves, but what we see in them inspires us to go where they have led the way.

In my early twenties, I was befriended by a wonderful group of young adults in their thirties. I was single and a senior in college; they were in the throes of early marriage and child rearing. We were all part of a small Christian community with a passionate commitment to serve homeless people in our city. I so admired my older friends and I wanted nothing more than to be where they were in life. They were more than happy to adopt me into their tribe as a younger sibling. I eventually realized, however, that I couldn't leapfrog over my twenties and land where they were. I had to live my life, which, in time, meant leaving my friends and the city where I attended college to find my way through that turbulent, formative decade. I didn't want to leave the warmth of their community and the identity I yearned to have among them. It was their example that motivated me to go.

Jesus was a master at using inspiring examples as an encouragement to those around him. His most famous parable was told in part to inspire a young lawyer to live according to the highest aspirations of love found in the teachings of scripture. The lawyer had approached Jesus to ask what he needed to do to inherit eternal life. Jesus knew the lawyer already knew the answer to his own question, so he asked him to recite the most foundational spiritual requirement found in the Torah, and the lawyer dutifully replied, "You shall the love the Lord your God will all your heart, mind, soul and strength. And love your neighbor as yourself."

"You are correct," Jesus told him. "Do that and you will live."

The lawyer pressed further, wanting Jesus to tell him exactly which neighbor he was required to love, presumably so that he wouldn't waste energy loving the wrong people. Jesus responds with the story we know as the Good Samaritan, in which a man is beaten and left for dead on the side of road. Three men see him; two continue on before one stops to help. The two passersby, to make the point even clearer, were righteous men in the eyes of the law. The man who stopped to help was of a despised race. Jesus then asks the lawyer which of the three men inspired him with his love for neighbor. When the lawyer answers, "The man who showed compassion," Jesus simply said, "Go and do likewise" (Luke 10:25–37).

Some of the questions to ask when discerning God's call are: Who inspires you? What would it look like for you to follow their example? If it seems impossible to go where they are, might it be that they are your guiding light, directing you through their inspiration where God is calling you to go? This power of inspiration is at work not only for us as individuals, but also in community. I often ask church leaders that are trying to discern future direction, "Is there a church nearby that is doing what you wish your church could do, that is reaching the people you wish you could reach?" If so, be inspired by their example, and learn from them. In your own way, as Jesus said, go and do likewise.

The Path of Joy

There is another way that we can experience God's call to go, one that is completely different from that of resistance or struggle. Sometimes, incredibly enough, God calls us to the very places where we ourselves most want to go. Sometimes God guides us toward our heart's greatest desire. There is so much in the spiritual life that asks us to accept what we cannot change and bravely set our faces toward the places that scare us, but there is also the experience of joy, of being led to places that are where we know we're supposed to be.

The path of joy, of our heart's desire, can be trusted. God gave us our desires to help guide us in life. Sometimes we're prevented from fulfilling those desires, for reasons that are beyond our understanding or control, but when the path opens to us, we are meant to take it. What a gift it is to go, in the words of Frederick Buechner, "to the place where our deep gladness and the world's deep hunger meet."[3]

I'll never forget the time a colleague said to me, as he was poised to make a dramatic change in his vocation, "I have been preparing my whole life for this moment." He was at least twenty years older than I was, and I couldn't imagine myself ever being at a similar stage in my life. I was in complete awe of his self-knowledge and certitude. I knew that I wanted to be able to say the same thing about my vocation someday. But just as in my twenties when I saw a life that I longed for but was not ready to live, I realized I would not be able to live my heart's desire without knowing how the many strands of my life would come together in the future.

There is one final dimension of going to consider here: those times when we are called to go while staying right where we are. In other words, God may be calling us to a new place, spiritually, relationally, or vocationally, yet to remain in place physically. This is the call to depth and maturity. In the wise words of Joan Chittister, "It may be the neighborhood we live in rather than the neighborhood we want that will really make human beings of us. It may be the job we have rather than the position we are selling our souls to get that may finally liberate us from ourselves."[4] Or in the words of Pastor Mark Batterson, "If Jesus isn't calling you out on the water, stay in the boat."[5]

---

3. Frederick Buechner, *Wishful Thinking: A Seeker's ABCs* (New York: Harper One, 1993), 119.

4. Joan Chittister, O.S.B, *The Rule of Benedict: Insights for the Ages* (New York: Crossroad Publishing, 1992).

5. Transcript from a podcast conversation between Mark Batterson and Carey Nieuwhof, *https://careynieuwhof.com/episode128/* (accessed February 14, 2019).

Much of my adult life has been defined by "going in place," staying put and listening for God's call to go and grow where I am. I didn't hear God call me to go to El Paso and stay there, for example, but to go and return to my life and engage the realities that journey taught me from where I am. There is a freedom that comes in going or staying as we feel called by God, in that we are responding, as best we can, to God. There is joy in Jesus's company, unlike anything else we can know, the joy of being with him, joining him in his ways of love. Thus however we sense the call to go—be it to places that frighten or inspire us, those we would choose gladly or do anything to avoid, to travel across boundaries or to physically stay put and to deepen where we are—we do not go alone. Jesus goes with us. Indeed, he goes before us and remains with us. Even when we say no, he stays at our side, and in the ways of grace, moves us from no to yes.

7

⌣

To Rest

RECEIVE THE GIFT
OF GOD'S GRACE, PEACE,
AND RESTORATION

> The apostles gathered around Jesus and told him all that
> they had done and taught. He said to them, "Come away
> to a deserted place all by yourselves and rest a while." For
> many were coming and going, and they had no leisure even
> to eat. And they went away in the boat to a deserted place
> by themselves. —Mark 6: 30–32

WHEN OUR SONS WERE TEN and seven years old, respectively,
I traveled with our older son, Amos, to Central America. We spent
three weeks in Guatemala studying Spanish and living with a host
family. Near the end of our time there, Paul and and our younger
son Patrick met us for a few days, and as a family we journeyed to
Honduras to visit the home for abandoned boys where Paul and I
had worked when we were first married.

As adults, Amos and Patrick have positive memories of our
travels, but at the time, it was a far more stressful experience than
I had anticipated. Amos had a hard time adjusting to the environment, the food, and being away from his friends. While we lived
comfortably, we were confronted daily with pervasive poverty that

as a parent I could not easily explain. More than once, Amos got sick, and he would plead with me to take him home. Thus, I lived in a constant state of worry. In my anxiety, I worked to keep us both really busy. I never relaxed.

When Paul and Patrick arrived, I was in that frenetic mode, with our days planned to the minute. Paul went along with this at first, but when I suggested on our last day in Guatemala that we take the boys to a tourist hotel with a swimming pool, he had finally had enough. "Just stop," he said. "I just want to be here with you and the boys. That's enough." Only then did I realize that my constant activity had kept me from being fully present to my family and to our experience in that beautiful, troubled country. I certainly wasn't present to God.

If only this story were the exception rather than the rule of my life, but in truth I have always had a hard time believing that being present is enough when there might be something more that I could do.

There's a story in the gospels of two sisters, Mary and Martha. They and their brother Lazarus were among Jesus's closest friends, and he would often slip away to spend time in their home. In a classic story of contrasts, we're told of a time when Jesus went to stay with his friends. As Jesus gathered in a room presumably with a group of men, Mary took the initiative to join them, sitting at Jesus's feet, taking in every word. Meanwhile, Martha busied herself in the kitchen preparing food for all the guests. At some point, Martha began resenting her sister's absence from the kitchen and complained to Jesus, asking him tell Mary to help her. Jesus instead tenderly spoke to Martha. "You are worried and distracted by many things; there is need of only one thing. Mary has chosen the better part, which will not be taken away from her" (Luke 10:38–42).

We come now to the last of the seven practices in the Way of Love: to rest. For some of us, it's hard to believe that rest "counts" because it doesn't feel like a practice to stop. The wisdom of the Way of Love is that rest is as essential a practice as any other, for in rest we learn what it means to enjoy our lives, relish in the beauty of creation, and savor the love of God.

The inability to rest is pervasive. In the summer of 2018, I surveyed members of the diocese of Washington to ask which practices in the Way of Love came easily for them and with which did they struggle. Nearly everyone who responded said that rest was the most difficult. "I'm not good at resting," one confessed. "I was raised to work," wrote another. "I'm not sure I know how to rest." More poignantly, in workshops we've held across the diocese on the topic of elder spirituality, many people in their seventies and eighties acknowledged how hard it is to let go of an identity predominantly defined by accomplishments or productivity. Resting can feel like giving up, or like loss. "Don't ever stop working," my mother said to me recently. "Life becomes so empty."

One reason I am so drawn to the Way of Love is precisely that I struggle with several of its practices. The discipline of practice, even when I must start over again and again, has a quiet and transformative impact on my life. Only in the spirit of confession, do I, arguably among the least qualified people on the planet, dare to write about rest.

I begin with gratitude to God who calls upon each of us to rest—not as a suggestion, but as an imperative. Rest is something we must do in order to live an abundant life. The commandment to rest goes all the way back to the beginnings of our faith tradition, a beginning Christians share with Jews and Muslims, as recorded in the biblical stories of creation. In the first of two creation stories found in Genesis, God created the heavens and the earth, all the creatures of the earth, and humankind in six days. The text then tells us that God rested on the seventh day, and in so doing created a day of rest (Gen. 1:1–2:3).

The creation story celebrates what our bodies tell us every day: we were created as mortal beings with a physical requirement to rest. We cannot survive long without physical rest. God's commandment isn't meant to be yet one more rule to adhere to in a legalistic life; rather, its purpose is that we might experience rest as a gift for our souls and bodies.

We aren't meant to work all the time. Should we forget that, our bodies may force us to rest by getting sick. That happened to our elder son Amos not long ago. He had been working very hard at his job, staying at the office late each night and working on weekends from home. My husband and I had come to town to visit and taken all our family out to dinner. From this meal, he and his wife contracted a serious bout of food poisoning. For three days he could barely move. It was that meal, and not exhaustion, that had made him sick. But being sick forced him to stop his frenetic pace, and when he recovered, he wrote to me, "While I can't remember ever being that sick in my life, I learned something through the experience. I learned that I need more rest." Since then he's made a few changes, nothing drastic, but enough to make room in his life for more rest and even a bit of play.

Practicing Sabbath

Sabbath is the word we use to describe God's call to rest, from the Hebrew, *shabbat*. The Jewish feast of Shabbat is patterned on the seventh day of creation when God rested. From Jewish tradition, we've inherited this notion of a day of rest—a full day. If you've ever experienced Shabbat in a Jewish home, you know that it begins on Friday evening with a lavish, celebratory, candlelit meal, complete with prayers, song, and laughter. Then all the next day, Saturday, for practicing Jews there is a restriction against work of any kind. It's a day for joy, for family and friends, and in the beautiful words of Rabbi Abraham Joshua Heschel, "to mend our tattered lives."[1]

---

1. Abraham Joshua Heschel, *The Sabbath* (New York: Ferrar, Straus & Giroux, 1951), 18.

My Jewish friends who practice Shabbat are quick to tell me that they're not rigid in their practice, taking to heart the old rabbinic teaching that Jesus himself quoted when the Pharisees criticized him for healing on the Sabbath: "The sabbath was made for humankind; not humankind for the sabbath" (Mark 2:27). If the call to rest becomes one more obligation to fulfill—and an impossible one at that—or one that keeps us from acts of compassion, or makes us feel guilty when we must work on a day of rest, then it is no longer the gift that God intends but yet another way we berate ourselves for not being sufficiently spiritual. In both Jewish and Christian tradition, the observance of Sabbath is not ultimately an act of obedience but rather an experience of freedom. God did not rest on the seventh day after creation in observance of any law. Rather, the scriptures and sacred interpretations of them for centuries have pointed out that God rested because God chose rest, to bask in the delight of creation.

Sometimes what needs to be done overrides the call to rest. It is not kind to chide parents of infant children, for example, that they aren't getting enough rest. What they need when rest is impossible is compassion and concrete expressions of help. The same is true for those with unforgiving demands at work or school, and those carrying a heavy load for others. As we're reminded in the wisdom writings of the Jewish Scriptures, "For everything there is a season, and a time for every matter under heaven" (Eccles. 3:1).

There is also provision in Jewish Sabbath practice for breaking the call to rest, particularly when a person's life is in danger. In Jesus we see someone who clearly embodies this principle of the primacy of life, for he never shirked when called upon to do good on the Sabbath, even if it involved work. Story after story in the gospels tell of him healing on the Sabbath, in direct violation of the strict enforcement of Jewish teachings. He sometimes deliberately violated Sabbath teachings in the presence of religious leaders, who were quick to criticize him, as a way of demonstrating the Sabbath's true meaning. In one of those stories, Jesus entered a village synagogue on the Sabbath and saw a man with a withered hand. A group of Pharisees, a particularly righteous sect, stood around to see what he would do. Jesus called the man with the withered hand and asked those standing by, "Is it lawful to do good or to do harm on the sabbath, to save life or to kill?" No one dared say anything. Jesus could barely contain his anger at the religious leaders' hardness of heart. "Stretch out your hand," Jesus told the wounded man, and when he did so, his hand was restored (Mark 3:1–6).

Prayer and Rest

Jesus also took time to rest. The gospels describe how he would go off to quiet places by himself or with his closest friends. There he would pray and restore his soul. When his rest was interrupted by a presenting need, he sacrificed his own needs in order to serve others. When the work was done, he would return to his practice of rest.

The Gospel of Mark tells of the time when Jesus and the disciples had been hard at work, teaching and healing throughout the Galilean countryside. It had been so intense for so long that they hadn't even had a chance to eat. I have had times like that; I suspect we all have. It was also, according to the text, when Jesus learned of John the Baptist's brutal murder at the hands of King Herod. Thus, he was also deeply grieving.

"Come away to a deserted place," he encouraged his disciples, "and rest a while." They got into a boat and set sail for the other side of the lake. But a large crowd saw where Jesus and his disciples were going. They hurried on foot and somehow managed to arrive on the other side of the lake ahead of Jesus and the disciples. When Jesus saw the desperation in the crowd, he put aside his need to rest and spent the day teaching and healing. Without complaint, the disciples worked at his side.

At the end of the day, when the disciples were at the limits of their strength and energy, they wanted Jesus to dismiss the crowd so that they might go and find food to eat. Instead, Jesus told them to feed the hungry crowd. They only had a few fish and some bread to offer, but Jesus asked for what they had, and from that offering that Jesus blessed before God, the multitudes were fed to satisfaction, with food left over.

As I wrote in an earlier chapter, I live my life inside the miracle of the loaves and fish, as we all do. God consistently and compassionately gives us the strength to carry on when we are at or have surpassed our limits, so that we can show up when we're tired and be present for those who need us. There's something deeply restorative in that experience, even restful, knowing that God can accomplish in us, as Paul writes, far more than we can ask for or imagine. The story, however, doesn't end there. After Jesus dismissed the satisfied crowd, he allowed himself at last to feel his exhaustion. Dismissing even his disciples, telling them to go on without him, he went to the mountain alone to pray and restore his soul.

The person I meet for spiritual direction offered me a bit of wisdom recently regarding the tension between the presenting needs of others or of work and the spiritual imperative to rest. I was telling him about the work I often feel I must do on my weekly day off. The work feels important to me, I told him, and I don't mind doing it. In the case of emergencies or unexpected opportunities, it doesn't feel that there is a choice involved. Often projects require more time than I can give during my work week, and like so many, I feel the pressure to work during a designated time of rest. Generally I don't mind, but I am aware that rest remains elusive.

My spiritual director suggested that I bring the matter to God in prayer. When I feel compelled to work, called to put my own needs aside for the sake of other obligations, could I acknowledge before God both my need to rest and my sense that my work priorities should come first? I might ask God, he said, not only to give me strength but to gift me with Sabbath rest in the midst of the demands before me.

He then spoke a word of warning: "Pay attention to the pattern of your life. If the response to choose work over rest becomes habitual, you risk losing perspective and responding as if every call to work were urgent and necessary." Sometimes we need to choose rest, even when the call to keep working is urgent, for we are mortal. Our souls and bodies can only do so much. Moreover, there is the risk of forgetting our place. "Be still," God says through the words of the psalmist, "and know that I am God" (Ps. 46:10).

My spiritual director's warning got my attention. I habitually choose work over rest without giving much thought to what I am doing, making me susceptible to what some have called "the tyranny of the urgent." That habit, while fruitful at times, is costly to myself and others. I make poorer choices when I'm tired. I can lose perspective and operate more from adrenaline and anxiety than is healthy. Those closest to me often pay the price for my commitment to work. And I miss many opportunities for joy.

What would change in my life and yours if we dared to believe that in God's eyes, our need for rest, and indeed, the gift of rest, is a priority for our own sake? How differently might we live?

One way that I'm trying to live differently is to accept opportunities for rest when they arise. They may not come on a fixed schedule, but when they do, I try to accept them without anxiety or guilt, lay aside what is left undone, and relish the gift of rest and renewal.

I've also become more aware of my need for sleep. For years, I prided myself on needing only five to six hours of sleep per night. As I've aged, however, I recognize that I don't function well without at least seven hours of sleep. In those luminous times as I fall asleep at night and as I wake up in the morning, I try now to savor the transition, mindful of God's presence.

Sabbath as a mindset is one that I can bring into my work, my director reminded me. "Think of Sabbath as resting in the presence of God," he said. "In a work situation, it's wonderfully restoring to assume a restful, attentive posture, asking for God's illumination. In that way it's possible to rise from your work rejuvenated."

The Spaciousness of Time

One way to think of rest is through the lens of time, and how we experience time. So often we speak of time as our taskmaster, or as a commodity which is always in scarce supply. In times of rest, we sometimes speak of passing time, even killing time. Rest and true Sabbath, in contrast, are about the spaciousness of time, what Rabbi Heschel describes as the redemption of time. "Time," says Heschel, "is the heart of existence . . . there is a realm of time where the goal is not to have but to be, not to own but to give, not to subdue but to be in accord." "The higher goal of spiritual living," he reminds us, "is not to amass a wealth of information, but to face sacred moments."[2]

Rest brings us into spacious time—not time filled to the brim with endless work, nor lingering in boredom, nor killed by mindless activity, but the fullness of time, where we can be fully present to ourselves, to one another, and to our Creator.

I cannot yet speak to you from the experience of weekly Sabbath as I imagine it—a full day of rest that I hope one day to have as part of my spiritual practice. But I can speak of the restoring, restful smaller practices that help me redeem time and restore my tattered soul.

I know what some of those restful moments are for me. One can be as simple as lighting a candle before an evening meal, taking a deep breath, and savoring the moment of friends or family

---

2. Heschel, 6.

gathered at table. Another is to find rest in a quiet walk or an invigorating bicycle ride. It is restful and restorative for me whenever I can allow time to drift, when I can let go, even for a moment, of the need to be productive.

It's been said that there is more to life than increasing its speed. We intrinsically mean more to God than what we feel we must do. To realize that for God rest is delight without distraction surely has the power to shift our perspective on the balance between our work and rest—even if only a little bit. Perhaps we can trust that what the Book of Common Prayer encourages us to pray is actually true: that in returning and rest we shall be saved, in quietness and confidence shall be our strength.

EPILOGUE

THE POET DAVID WHYTE tells the story of an old Irish monk standing alone at the edge of the monastic precinct. When he hears the church bell toll, calling him to prayer, he says to himself, "That is the most beautiful sound in the world." But then the monk hears a blackbird calling from out in a field, and he says to himself, "That's also the most beautiful sound in the world."[1] What the two experiences have in common is the call itself, which is both an invitation and a summons. In a poem entitled, "The Bell and the Blackbird," Whyte describes a life in which these two calls are in constant conversation. "Either way," he reminds us, "takes courage."[2]

At the heart of the Way of Love is Jesus's call to us, an invitation to go deep within ourselves to experience his unfailing, unconditional love and to go out, where we can both offer and experience that same love in relationship with others. Like our experience of time, and of life itself, Jesus's way is both a journey and an invitation to be still in the presence of God.

I pray that these reflections have been an encouragement for you as you listen for the unique and wondrous ways that Jesus might be calling you, first to know how prized you are in the eyes of God and how much Jesus himself enjoys spending time in your

---

1. *https://onbeing.org/programs/poetry-from-the-on-being-gathering-david-whyte-opening-night-sep2018/.*

2. David Whyte, "The Bell and the Blackbird," in *The Bell and the Blackbird* (Langley, WA: Many Rivers Press, 2018), 23.

company. And I pray that you hear his call to consider how in your wondrous and gifted life to join in his love for others and for our world.

This is a time of tremendous spiritual creativity in the Episcopal Church, and there is a growing body of resources available to help us all answer Jesus's call. The Episcopal Church website, *https://www.episcopalchurch.org/way-of-love*, serves as a repository of those resources, even as it reminds us that the Way of Love is more than program or a curriculum, but a way of life.

We are blessed as we walk this way together.

APPENDIX

The Way of Love Lectionary

The Episcopal Diocese of Washington developed a lectionary to introduce the Way of Love and seven practices for a Jesus-centered life.[1] An introduction and eight Propers were collected as a means for congregations in the diocese to begin to explore the Way of Love.

Introduction
TO HAVE A RULE OF LIFE

OPENING COLLECT
Gracious God, in you we live and move and have our being: We humbly pray you so to guide and govern us by your Holy Spirit, that in all the cares and occupations of our life we may not forget you, but may remember that we are ever walking in your sight; through Jesus Christ our Lord. *Amen.* (For Quiet Confidence)[2]

---

1. Prepared by the Rt. Rev. Mariann Budde, Bishop of Washington; the Rev. Dr. Patricia Lyons, Missioner for Evangelism and Community Engagement; the Rev. Richard Weinberg, Strategic Communications Advisor; and the Rev. Daryl Paul Lobban, Missioner for Communications (Episcopal Diocese of Washington, 2018). Used with permission.

2. Book of Common Prayer, 832.

SCRIPTURE

Isaiah 55:1–3, 6–11

Ho, everyone who thirsts, come to the waters; and you that have no money, come, buy and eat! Come, buy wine and milk without money and without price.

Why do you spend your money for that which is not bread, and your labor for that which does not satisfy? Listen carefully to me, and eat what is good, and delight yourselves in rich food. Incline your ear, and come to me; listen, so that you may live. I will make with you an everlasting covenant, my steadfast, sure love for David.

Seek the Lord while he may be found, call upon him while he is near; let the wicked forsake their way, and the unrighteous their thoughts; let them return to the Lord, that he may have mercy on them, and to our God, for he will abundantly pardon. For my thoughts are not your thoughts, nor are your ways my ways, says the Lord. For as the heavens are higher than the earth, so are my ways higher than your ways and my thoughts than your thoughts. For as the rain and the snow come down from heaven, and do not return there until they have watered the earth, making it bring forth and sprout, giving seed to the sower and bread to the eater, so shall my word be that goes out from my mouth; it shall not return to me empty, but it shall accomplish that which I purpose, and succeed in the thing for which I sent it.

Psalm 19:7–14

The law of the Lord is perfect,
   reviving the soul;
the decrees of the Lord are sure,
   making wise the simple;
the precepts of the Lord are right,
   rejoicing the heart;
the commandment of the Lord is clear,
   enlightening the eyes;
the fear of the Lord is pure,
   enduring forever;

the ordinances of the Lord are true
   and righteous altogether.
More to be desired are they than gold,
   even much fine gold;
sweeter also than honey,
   and drippings of the honeycomb.
Moreover by them is your servant warned;
   in keeping them there is great reward.
But who can detect their errors?
   Clear me from hidden faults.
Keep back your servant also from the insolent;
   do not let them have dominion over me.
Then I shall be blameless,
   and innocent of great transgression.
Let the words of my mouth and the meditation of my heart
   be acceptable to you,
   O Lord, my rock and my redeemer.

Romans 12:1–2

I appeal to you therefore, brothers and sisters, by the mercies of God, to present your bodies as a living sacrifice, holy and acceptable to God, which is your spiritual worship. Do not be conformed to this world, but be transformed by the renewing of your minds, so that you may discern what is the will of God—what is good and acceptable and perfect.

John 15:1–11

I am the true vine, and my Father is the vine-grower. He removes every branch in me that bears no fruit. Every branch that bears fruit he prunes to make it bear more fruit. You have already been cleansed by the word that I have spoken to you. Abide in me as I abide in you. Just as the branch cannot bear fruit by itself unless it abides in the vine, neither can you unless you abide in me. I am the vine, you are the branches. Those who abide in me and I in them bear much fruit, because apart from me you can do nothing. Whoever does not abide in me is thrown away like a branch and withers; such branches are gathered, thrown into the fire, and burned. If you abide in me, and my words abide in you, ask for whatever you wish, and it will be done for you. My Father is glorified by this, that you bear much fruit and become my disciples. As the Father has loved me, so I have loved you; abide in my love. If you keep my commandments, you will abide in my love, just as I have kept my Father's commandments and abide in his love. I have said these things to you so that my joy may be in you, and that your joy may be complete.

Turn

CHOOSE TO FOLLOW JESUS

OPENING COLLECT

O God, whose glory it is always to have mercy: Be gracious to all who have gone astray from your ways, and bring them again with penitent hearts and steadfast faith to embrace and hold fast the unchangeable truth of your Word, Jesus Christ your Son; who with you and the Holy Spirit lives and reigns, one God, for ever and ever. *Amen.* (2 Lent)[3]

SCRIPTURE

Exodus 3:1–6

Moses was keeping the flock of his father-in-law Jethro, the priest of Midian; he led his flock beyond the wilderness, and came to Horeb, the mountain of God. There the angel of the Lord appeared to him in a flame of fire out of a bush; he looked, and the bush was blazing, yet it was not consumed. Then Moses said, "I must turn aside and look at this great sight, and see why the bush is not burned up." When the Lord saw that he had turned aside to see, God called to him out of the bush, "Moses, Moses!" And he said, "Here I am." Then he said, "Come no closer! Remove the sandals from your feet, for the place on which you are standing is holy ground." He said further, "I am the God of your father, the God of Abraham, the God of Isaac, and the God of Jacob." And Moses hid his face, for he was afraid to look at God.

---

3. Book of Common Prayer, 218.

Psalm 119:169–176

Let my cry come before you, O Lord;
   give me understanding according to your word.
Let my supplication come before you;
   deliver me according to your promise.
My lips will pour forth praise,
   because you teach me your statutes.
My tongue will sing of your promise,
   for all your commandments are right.
Let your hand be ready to help me,
   for I have chosen your precepts.
I long for your salvation, O Lord,
   and your law is my delight.
Let me live that I may praise you,
   and let your ordinances help me.
I have gone astray like a lost sheep; seek out your servant,
   for I do not forget your commandments.

2 Corinthians 4:5–7

For we do not proclaim ourselves; we proclaim Jesus Christ as Lord and ourselves as your slaves for Jesus' sake. For it is the God who said, "Let light shine out of darkness," who has shone in our hearts to give the light of the knowledge of the glory of God in the face of Jesus Christ. But we have this treasure in clay jars, so that it may be made clear that this extraordinary power belongs to God and does not come from us.

Luke 5:1–11

Once while Jesus was standing beside the lake of Gennesaret, and the crowd was pressing in on him to hear the word of God, he saw two boats there at the shore of the lake; the fishermen had gone out of them and were washing their nets. He got into one of the boats, the one belonging to Simon, and asked him to put out a little way from the shore. Then he sat down and taught the crowds from the boat. When he had finished speaking, he said to Simon, "Put out into the deep water and let down your nets for a catch." Simon answered, "Master, we have worked all night long but have caught nothing. Yet if you say so, I will let down the nets." When they had done this, they caught so many fish that their nets were beginning to break. So they signaled their partners in the other boat to come and help them. And they came and filled both boats, so that they began to sink. But when Simon Peter saw it, he fell down at Jesus' knees, saying, "Go away from me, Lord, for I am a sinful man!" For he and all who were with him were amazed at the catch of fish that they had taken; and so also were James and John, sons of Zebedee, who were partners with Simon.

Then Jesus said to Simon, "Do not be afraid; from now on you will be catching people." When they had brought their boats to shore, they left everything and followed him.

Learn

REFLECT ON SCRIPTURE EACH DAY, ESPECIALLY ON JESUS'S LIFE AND TEACHINGS

OPENING COLLECT

Grant us, Lord, not to be anxious about earthly things, but to love things heavenly; and even now, while we are placed among things that are passing away, to hold fast to those that shall endure; through Jesus Christ our Lord, who lives and reigns with you and the Holy Spirit, one God, for ever and ever. *Amen.* (Proper 20)[4]

SCRIPTURE

Micah 4:1–5

In days to come
    the mountain of the Lord's house
shall be established as the highest of the mountains,
    and shall be raised up above the hills.

---

4. Book of Common Prayer, 234.

Peoples shall stream to it,
    and many nations shall come and say:
"Come, let us go up to the mountain of the Lord,
    to the house of the God of Jacob;
that he may teach us his ways
    and that we may walk in his paths."
For out of Zion shall go forth instruction,
    and the word of the Lord from Jerusalem.
He shall judge between many peoples,
    and shall arbitrate between strong nations far away;
they shall beat their swords into plowshares,
    and their spears into pruning-hooks;
nation shall not lift up sword against nation,
    neither shall they learn war any more;
but they shall all sit under their own vines and under their own fig trees,
    and no one shall make them afraid;
    for the mouth of the Lord of hosts has spoken.
For all the peoples walk,
    each in the name of its god,
but we will walk in the name of the Lord our God
    for ever and ever.

Psalm 90:1–12

Lord you have been our dwelling place
    in all generations.
Before the mountains were brought forth,
    or ever you had formed the earth and the world,
    from everlasting to everlasting you are God.
You turn us back to dust
    and say, "Turn back, you mortals."
For a thousand years in your sight
    are like yesterday when it is past,
    or like a watch in the night.
You sweep them away; they are like a dream,
    like the grass that is renewed in the morning;

in the morning it flourishes and is renewed;
  in the evening it fades and withers.
For we are consumed by your anger;
  by your wrath we are overwhelmed.
You have set our iniquities before you,
  our secret sins in the light of your countenance.
For all our days pass away under your wrath;
  our years come to an end like a sigh.
The days of our life are seventy years,
  Or perhaps eighty, if we are strong;
  even their span is only toil and trouble;
  they are soon gone, and we fly away.
Who considers the power of your anger?
  Your wrath is as great as the fear that is due you.
So teach us to count our days
  that we may gain a wise heart.

Hebrews 4:12–16

Indeed, the word of God is living and active, sharper than any two-edged sword, piercing until it divides soul from spirit, joints from marrow; it is able to judge the thoughts and intentions of the heart. And before him no creature is hidden, but all are naked and laid bare to the eyes of the one to whom we must render an account. Since, then, we have a great high priest who has passed through the heavens, Jesus, the Son of God, let us hold fast to our confession. For we do not have a high priest who is unable to sympathize with our weaknesses, but we have one who in every respect has been tested as we are, yet without sin. Let us therefore approach the throne of grace with boldness, so that we may receive mercy and find grace to help in time of need.

Matthew 13:44–53

"The kingdom of heaven is like treasure hidden in a field, which someone found and hid; then in his joy he goes and sells all that he has and buys that field. Again, the kingdom of heaven is like a merchant in search of fine pearls; on finding one pearl of great value, he went and sold all that he had and bought it. Again, the kingdom of heaven is like a net that was thrown into the sea and caught fish of every kind; when it was full, they drew it ashore, sat down, and put the good into baskets but threw out the bad. So it will be at the end of the age. The angels will come out and separate the evil from the righteous and throw them into the furnace of fire, where there will be weeping and gnashing of teeth. Have you understood all this?" They answered, "Yes." And he said to them, "Therefore every scribe who has been trained for the kingdom of heaven is like the master of a household who brings out of his treasure what is new and what is old." When Jesus had finished these parables, he left that place.

Pray

DWELL INTENTIONALLY WITH GOD DAILY

OPENING COLLECT

Almighty and everlasting God, you are always more ready to hear than we to pray, and to give more than we either desire or deserve: Pour upon us the abundance of your mercy, forgiving us those things of which our conscience is afraid, and giving us those good things for which we are not worthy to ask, except through the merits and mediation of Jesus Christ our Savior; who lives and reigns with you and the Holy Spirit, one God, for ever and ever. *Amen.* (Proper 22)[5]

SCRIPTURE

1 Samuel 3:1–10

Now the boy Samuel was ministering to the Lord under Eli. The word of the Lord was rare in those days; visions were not widespread. At that time Eli, whose eyesight had begun to grow dim so that he could not see, was lying down in his room; the lamp of God had not yet gone out, and Samuel was lying down in the temple of the Lord, where the ark of God was. Then the Lord called, "Samuel! Samuel!" and he said, "Here I am!" and ran to Eli, and said, "Here I am, for

---

5. Ibid., 234.

you called me." But he said, "I did not call; lie down again." So he went and lay down. The Lord called again, "Samuel!" Samuel got up and went to Eli, and said, "Here I am, for you called me." But he said, "I did not call, my son; lie down again." Now Samuel did not yet know the Lord, and the word of the Lord had not yet been revealed to him. The Lord called Samuel again, a third time. And he got up and went to Eli, and said, "Here I am, for you called me." Then Eli perceived that the Lord was calling the boy.

Therefore Eli said to Samuel, "Go, lie down; and if he calls you, you shall say, 'Speak, Lord, for your servant is listening.'" So Samuel went and lay down in his place. Now the Lord came and stood there, calling as before, "Samuel! Samuel!" And Samuel said, "Speak, for your servant is listening."

Psalm 25:1–10

To you, O Lord, I lift up my soul.
O my God, in you I trust;
    do not let me be put to shame;
    do not let my enemies exult over me.
Do not let those who wait for you be put to shame;
    let them be ashamed who are wantonly treacherous.
Make me to know your ways, O Lord;
    teach me your paths.
Lead me in your truth, and teach me,
    for you are the God of my salvation;
    for you I wait all day long.
Be mindful of your mercy, O Lord, and of your steadfast love,
    for they have been from of old.
Do not remember the sins of my youth or my transgressions;
    according to your steadfast love remember me,
    for your goodness' sake, O Lord!
Good and upright is the Lord;
    therefore he instructs sinners in the way.
He leads the humble in what is right,
    and teaches the humble his way.

All the paths of the Lord are steadfast love and faithfulness,
   for those who keep his covenant and his decrees.

2 Corinthians 12:7–10

Therefore, to keep me from being too elated, a thorn was given me in the flesh, a messenger of Satan to torment me, to keep me from being too elated. Three times I appealed to the Lord about this, that it would leave me, but he said to me, "My grace is sufficient for you, for power is made perfect in weakness." So, I will boast all the more gladly of my weaknesses, so that the power of Christ may dwell in me. Therefore I am content with weaknesses, insults, hardships, persecutions, and calamities for the sake of Christ; for whenever I am weak, then I am strong.

Luke 11:1–13

Jesus was praying in a certain place, and after he had finished, one of his disciples said to him, "Lord, teach us to pray, as John taught his disciples." He said to them, "When you pray, say: Father, hallowed be your name. Your kingdom come. Give us each day our daily bread. And forgive us our sins, for we ourselves forgive everyone indebted to us. And do not bring us to the time of trial." And he said to them, "Suppose one of you has a friend, and you go to him at midnight and say to him, 'Friend, lend me three loaves of bread; for a friend of mine has arrived, and I have nothing to set before him.' And he answers from within, 'Do not bother me; the door has already been locked, and my children are with me in bed; I cannot get up and give you anything.' I tell you, even though he will not get up and give him anything because he is his friend, at least because of his persistence he will get up and give him whatever he needs. So I say to you, Ask, and it will be given you; search, and you will find; knock, and the door will be opened for you. For everyone who asks receives, and everyone who searches finds, and for everyone who knocks, the door will be opened. Is there anyone among you who, if your child asks for a fish, will give a snake instead of a fish? Or if the child asks for an egg, will give a scorpion? If you then, who are evil, know how to give good gifts to your children, how much more will the heavenly Father give the Holy Spirit to those who ask him!"

Worship
GATHER IN COMMUNITY WEEKLY

OPENING COLLECT
O God, whose blessed Son made himself known to his disciples in the breaking of bread: Open the eyes of our faith, that we may behold him in all his redeeming work; who lives and reigns with you, in the unity of the Holy Spirit, one God, now and forever. *Amen.* (Third Sunday of Easter)[6]

SCRIPTURE
Isaiah 56:1–7
Thus says the Lord:
    Maintain justice, and do what is right,
for soon my salvation will come,
    and my deliverance be revealed.
Happy is the mortal who does this,
    the one who holds it fast,
who keeps the sabbath, not profaning it,
    and refrains from doing any evil.
Do not let the foreigner joined to the Lord say,
    "The Lord will surely separate me from his people";
and do not let the eunuch say,
    "I am just a dry tree."
For thus says the Lord:
To the eunuchs who keep my sabbaths,
    who choose the things that please me
    and hold fast my covenant,
I will give, in my house and within my walls,
    a monument and a name better than sons and daughters;
I will give them an everlasting name
    that shall not be cut off.

---

6. Ibid., 224–225.

And the foreigners who join themselves to the Lord,
  to minister to him, to love the name of the Lord,
  and to be his servants,
all who keep the sabbath, and do not profane it,
  and hold fast my covenant—
these I will bring to my holy mountain,
  and make them joyful in my house of prayer;
their burnt-offerings and their sacrifices
  will be accepted on my altar;
for my house shall be called a house of prayer
  for all peoples.

Psalm 96:1–9

O sing to the Lord a new song;
  sing to the Lord, all the earth.
Sing to the Lord, bless his name;
  tell of his salvation from day to day.
Declare his glory among the nations,
  his marvelous works among all the peoples.
For great is the Lord, and greatly to be praised;
  he is to be revered above all gods.
For all the gods of the peoples are idols,
  but the Lord made the heavens.
Honor and majesty are before him;
  strength and beauty are in his sanctuary.
Ascribe to the Lord, O families of the peoples,
  ascribe to the Lord glory and strength.
Ascribe to the Lord the glory due his name;
  bring an offering, and come into his courts.
Worship the Lord in holy splendor;
  tremble before him, all the earth.

1 Corinthians 11:23–26

For I received from the Lord what I also handed on to you, that the Lord Jesus on the night when he was betrayed took a loaf of bread, and when he had given thanks, he broke it and said, "This is my body that is for you. Do this in remembrance of me." In the same way he took the cup also, after supper, saying, "This cup is the new covenant in my blood. Do this, as often as you drink it, in remembrance of me." For as often as you eat this bread and drink the cup, you proclaim the Lord's death until he comes.

Luke 24:28–35

As they came near the village to which they were going, he walked ahead as if he were going on. But they urged him strongly, saying, "Stay with us, because it is almost evening and the day is now nearly over." So he went in to stay with them. When he was at the table with them, he took bread, blessed and broke it, and gave it to them. Then their eyes were opened, and they recognized him; and he vanished from their sight. They said to each other, "Were not our hearts burning within us while he was talking to us on the road, while he was opening the scriptures to us?" That same hour they got up and returned to Jerusalem; and they found the eleven and their companions gathered together. They were saying, "The Lord has risen indeed, and he has appeared to Simon!" Then they told what had happened on the road, and how he had been made known to them in the breaking of the bread.

Bless
TO BLESS THE SPACE BETWEEN US
TO BE PEOPLE OF BLESSING

OPENING COLLECT

O God, from whom all good proceeds: Grant that by your inspiration we may think those things that are right, and by your merciful guiding may do them; through Jesus Christ our Lord, who lives and reigns with you and the Holy Spirit, one God, for ever and ever. *Amen.* (Proper 5)[7]

---

7. Ibid., 229.

SCRIPTURE

Genesis 32:22–30

The same night he got up and took his two wives, his two maids, and his eleven children, and crossed the ford of the Jabbok. He took them and sent them across the stream, and likewise everything that he had. Jacob was left alone; and a man wrestled with him until daybreak. When the man saw that he did not prevail against Jacob, he struck him on the hip socket; and Jacob's hip was put out of joint as he wrestled with him. Then he said, "Let me go, for the day is breaking." But Jacob said, "I will not let you go, unless you bless me." So he said to him, "What is your name?" And he said, "Jacob." Then the man said, "You shall no longer be called Jacob, but Israel, for you have striven with God and with humans, and have prevailed." Then Jacob asked him, "Please tell me your name." But he said, "Why is it that you ask my name?" And there he blessed him. So Jacob called the place Peniel, saying, "For I have seen God face to face, and yet my life is preserved."

Psalm 23

The Lord is my shepherd, I shall not want.
　He makes me lie down in green pastures;
he leads me beside still waters;
　he restores my soul.
He leads me in right paths
　for his name's sake.
Even though I walk through the darkest valley,
　I fear no evil;
for you are with me;
　your rod and your staff—
　they comfort me.
You prepare a table before me
　in the presence of my enemies;
you anoint my head with oil;
　my cup overflows.
Surely goodness and mercy shall follow me
　all the days of my life,

and I shall dwell in the house of the Lord
my whole life long.

Romans 12:9–21

Let love be genuine; hate what is evil, hold fast to what is good; love one another with mutual affection; outdo one another in showing honor. Do not lag in zeal, be ardent in spirit, serve the Lord. Rejoice in hope, be patient in suffering, persevere in prayer. Contribute to the needs of the saints; extend hospitality to strangers.

Bless those who persecute you; bless and do not curse them. Rejoice with those who rejoice, weep with those who weep. Live in harmony with one another; do not be haughty, but associate with the lowly; do not claim to be wiser than you are. Do not repay anyone evil for evil, but take thought for what is noble in the sight of all. If it is possible, so far as it depends on you, live peaceably with all. Beloved, never avenge yourselves, but leave room for the wrath of God; for it is written, "Vengeance is mine, I will repay, says the Lord." No, "if your enemies are hungry, feed them; if they are thirsty, give them something to drink; for by doing this you will heap burning coals on their heads." Do not be overcome by evil, but overcome evil with good.

Matthew 25:31–40

When the Son of Man comes in his glory, and all the angels with him, then he will sit on the throne of his glory. All the nations will be gathered before him, and he will separate people one from another as a shepherd separates the sheep from the goats, and he will put the sheep at his right hand and the goats at the left. Then the king will say to those at his right hand, "Come, you that are blessed by my Father, inherit the kingdom prepared for you from the foundation of the world; for I was hungry and you gave me food, I was thirsty and you gave me something to drink, I was a stranger and you welcomed me, I was naked and you gave me clothing, I was sick and you took care of me, I was in prison and you visited me." Then the righteous will answer him, "Lord, when was it that we saw you hungry and gave you food, or thirsty and gave you something to drink? And when was it that we saw you a stranger and welcomed you, or naked and gave you clothing? And when was it that we saw you sick or in prison and visited you?" And the king will answer them, "Truly I tell you, just as you did it to one of the least of these who are members of my family, you did it to me."

Go

CROSS BOUNDARIES, LISTEN DEEPLY, AND LIVE LIKE JESUS

OPENING COLLECT

Lord, make us instruments of your peace. Where there is hatred, let us sow love; where there is injury, pardon; where there is discord, union; where there is doubt, faith; where there is despair, hope; where there is darkness, light; where there is sadness, joy. Grant that we may not so much seek to be consoled as to console; to be understood as to understand; to be loved as to love. For it is in giving that we receive; it is in pardoning that we are pardoned; and it is in dying that we are born to eternal life. Amen. (Prayer attributed to St. Francis)[8]

SCRIPTURE

Jonah 3:1–10

The word of the Lord came to Jonah a second time, saying, "Get up, go to Nineveh, that great city, and proclaim to it the message that I tell you." So Jonah set out and went to Nineveh, according to the word of the Lord. Now Nineveh was an exceedingly large city, a three days' walk across. Jonah began to go into the city, going a day's walk. And he cried out, "Forty days more, and Nineveh shall be overthrown!" And the people of Nineveh believed God; they proclaimed a fast, and everyone, great and small, put on sackcloth.

When the news reached the king of Nineveh, he rose from his throne, removed his robe, covered himself with sackcloth, and sat in ashes. Then he had a proclamation made in Nineveh: "By the decree

---

8. Ibid., 833.

of the king and his nobles: No human being or animal, no herd or flock, shall taste anything. They shall not feed, nor shall they drink water. Human beings and animals shall be covered with sackcloth, and they shall cry mightily to God. All shall turn from their evil ways and from the violence that is in their hands. Who knows? God may relent and change his mind; he may turn from his fierce anger, so that we do not perish." When God saw what they did, how they turned from their evil ways, God changed his mind about the calamity that he had said he would bring upon them; and he did not do it.

Psalm 41:1–4

Happy are those who consider the poor;
  the Lord delivers them in the day of trouble.
The Lord protects them and keeps them alive;
  they are called happy in the land.
You do not give them up to the will of their enemies.
The Lord sustains them on their sickbed;
  in their illness you heal all their infirmities.
As for me, I said, "O Lord, be gracious to me;
  heal me, for I have sinned against you."

1 John 3:11, 18–24

For this is the message you have heard from the beginning, that we should love one another. Little children, let us love, not in word or speech, but in truth and action. And by this we will know that we are from the truth and will reassure our hearts before him whenever our hearts condemn us; for God is greater than our hearts, and he knows everything. Beloved, if our hearts do not condemn us, we have boldness before God; and we receive from him whatever we ask, because we obey his commandments and do what pleases him. And this is his commandment, that we should believe in the name of his Son Jesus Christ and love one another, just as he has commanded us. All who obey his commandments abide in him, and he abides in them. And by this we know that he abides in us, by the Spirit that he has given us.

Luke 10:25–37

A lawyer stood up to test Jesus. "Teacher," he said, "what must I do to inherit eternal life?" He said to him, "What is written in the law? What do you read there?" He answered, "You shall love the Lord your God with all your heart, and with all your soul, and with all your strength, and with all your mind; and your neighbor as yourself." And he said to him, "You have given the right answer; do this, and you will live." But wanting to justify himself, he asked Jesus, "And who is my neighbor?" Jesus replied, "A man was going down from Jerusalem to Jericho, and fell into the hands of robbers, who stripped him, beat him, and went away, leaving him half dead. Now by chance a priest was going down that road; and when he saw him, he passed by on the other side. So likewise a Levite, when he came to the place and saw him, passed by on the other side. But a Samaritan while traveling came near him; and when he saw him, he was moved with pity. He went to him and bandaged his wounds, having poured oil and wine on them. Then he put him on his own animal, brought him to an inn, and took care of him. The next day he took out two denarii, gave them to the innkeeper, and said, 'Take care of him; and when I come back, I will repay you whatever more you spend.' Which of these three, do you think, was a neighbor to the man who fell into the hands of the robbers?" He said, "The one who showed him mercy." Jesus said to him, "Go and do likewise."

Rest

RECEIVE THE GIFT OF GOD'S GRACE, PEACE,
AND RESTORATION

OPENING COLLECT

O God of peace, who has taught us that in returning and rest we shall be saved, in quietness and confidence shall be our strength: By the might of your Spirit lift us, we pray, to your presence, where we may be still and know that you are God; through Jesus Christ our Lord. *Amen.*

SCRIPTURE

Exodus 20:8–11

Remember the sabbath day, and keep it holy. Six days you shall labor and do all your work. But the seventh day is a sabbath to the Lord your God; you shall not do any work—you, your son or your daughter, your male or female slave, your livestock, or the alien resident in your towns. For in six days the Lord made heaven and earth, the sea, and all that is in them, but rested the seventh day; therefore the Lord blessed the sabbath day and consecrated it.

Psalm 127: 1–2

Unless the Lord builds the house,
    those who build it labor in vain.
Unless the Lord guards the city,
    the guard keeps watch in vain.
It is in vain that you rise up early
    and go late to rest,
eating the bread of anxious toil;
    for he gives sleep to his beloved.

Philippians 4: 4–7

Rejoice in the Lord always; again I will say, Rejoice. Let your gentleness be known to everyone. The Lord is near. Do not worry about anything, but in everything by prayer and supplication with thanksgiving let your requests be made known to God. And the peace of God, which surpasses all understanding, will guard your hearts and your minds in Christ Jesus.

Matthew 11:28–30

Come to me, all you that are weary and are carrying heavy burdens, and I will give you rest. Take my yoke upon you, and learn from me; for I am gentle and humble in heart, and you will find rest for your souls. For my yoke is easy, and my burden is light.

Mark 6: 7–13, 30–32

Jesus called the twelve and began to send them out two by two, and gave them authority over the unclean spirits. He ordered them to take nothing for their journey except a staff; no bread, no bag, no money in their belts; but to wear sandals and not to put on two tunics. He said to them, "Wherever you enter a house, stay there until you leave the place. If any place will not welcome you and they refuse to hear you, as you leave, shake off the dust that is on your feet as a testimony against them." So they went out and proclaimed that all should repent. They cast out many demons, and anointed with oil many who were sick and cured them.

The apostles gathered around Jesus, and told him all that they had done and taught. He said to them, "Come away to a deserted place all by yourselves and rest a while." For many were coming and going, and they had no leisure even to eat. And they went away in the boat to a deserted place by themselves.

ACKNOWLEDGMENTS

I WOULD LIKE TO PUBLICLY thank Presiding Bishop Michael Curry for his passionate faith and leadership, and for urging all of us in the Episcopal Church to adopt Jesus's way of love as our spiritual rule of life.

I am indebted to the growing community of inspired teachers, preachers, and Way of Love practitioners across the Episcopal Church whose generous creativity is a blessing to us all.

Special thanks to the Rev. Canon Stephanie Spellers, Canon to the Presiding Bishop for Evangelism, Reconciliation, and Stewardship of Creation; Dr. Courtney Cowart, Executive Director, Society for the Increase of Ministry; and Ms. Sharon Ely Pearson, editor, Church Publishing Incorporated for their encouragement and assistance.

I also wish to acknowledge my colleagues in the Episcopal Diocese of Washington, including the clergy and lay leaders who have written their own fine reflections on the seven practices, led spiritual retreats, engaged in conversations, and have committed to practice the Way of Love in intentional ways. You are my inspiration.

A special word of thanks to several on the diocesan staff who were at my side as this adventure moved from sermon series to podcast to written publication: the Rev. Richard Weinberg, the Rev. Daryl Lobban, The Rev. Dr. Patricia Lyons, and Ms. Keely Thrall.

Finally, heartfelt thanks to my husband, Paul Budde, whose support and encouragement I rely on daily, and who is always there when I am weary to cheer me on.